CONDENSED VERSION

THE

TRUTH®

Acclaim for

THE TRUTH by AD Infinitum

"An exquisite exposition of the Universal Way"

— Michael Harmer, Esteemed Legal Crusader, Universalist and
Human Rights Campaigner

"We need to take the eternal truth message seriously, and act on it in our times. This book shows us how, and through it new life is possible. The enormity of it, the wholeness of it, the purity of it, is just astounding."

— Rev. Hannie Hoffman, Uniting Church Minister

"This is a truly remarkable book. It focuses on love and trust and knowing who you really are, so you can be part of this new movement to change the world. It is essential reading at this time on the planet."

— Dr. Ben-Zion Weiss, PhD, Spirituality Lecturer (University of
Western Sydney), Author

"Written with passion and power, this engaging book contains so much thought-provoking material that one reading is not enough to absorb all its wisdom. I think The Truth is an important book with the power to change the way we see ourselves so that we can enrich our lives."

— Diane Armstrong, Award-Winning Internationally Best Selling
Author and Journalist

"The only book we all must read! It is our responsibility, as adults, parents, educators or leaders, to prevent the increasing violence and destruction in the world. We need to purify our hearts, and to rediscover our consciousness. We must all wake up. And this book shows us how. WE ALL NEED THIS MESSAGE NOW...BEFORE IT'S TOO LATE!"

— Kate Pau, Teacher and Educator

"Simply put, this wonderful book makes you stop, think and re-evaluate what is really important and meaningful in this busy, crazy life we lead. It helps us become kinder and more compassionate to ourselves and those around us, promotes self-esteem and positive thinking and shows us the right path forward."

— Gillian French, Registered Nurse

CONDENSED VERSION

THE

TRUTH®

A BOOK BY
AD INFINITUM

Please Note: Names and details in some anecdotes and stories have been changed to protect the identity of the persons involved. The parts of the book that are indented and in italic were examples added to the original text, by the "conduit" or first messenger, for their own sense of clarity.

Every attempt has been made to represent copyright holders and to reference contributing authors' quotes. If there are any concerns or requested changes to references, please contact us at: www.thetruth.community.

The author of this book does not dispense medical advise or prescribe the use of any technique as a form of treatment for physical or medical problems without the advise of a physician, either directly or indirectly. The intent of this message is only to offer information of a general nature to help you in you quest for fulfillment, emotional and spiritual wellbeing, and to enable a united, peaceful world. In the event you use any of the information in this book for yourself, which is your constitutional right, the author and the publisher assume no responsibility for your actions.

The Truth®
Condensed Version (First Edition)

The Truth® was first published in 2015

THE TRUTH ®
Copyright © LM Jones 2015

ISBN 978-0-9943230-1-9
Printed Copy

Spread the word, share your stories, join the movement and stay connected at www.thetruth.community

This book is part of a global movement, so the utilization of this message is allowed and encouraged for the purposes of spreading the word and creating a new reality, provided the website www.thetruth.community and the book The Truth® by AD Infinitum are sited and linked. It is vital that this message remain uncorrupted and complete. Any distortion or misrepresentation of The Truth® and its message is forbidden.

*This book is dedicated to you, its reader and message bearer
and to the Incredible Source Energy from which you came.*

Proceeds from this book received by AD Infinitum will be used to
create awareness and freedom.

CONTENTS

Prologue

It would seem unethical for me to start this book without
acknowledging its author:
and that is not me.
The Truth was written through me,
and this is the most authentic and true description I can give you.
I had a strong calling to write this book for many years and believe I
was guided,
through incredible synchronicity, to undertake extensive university
study
– M.A. Social Ecology and M.Ed. (Transformative) Leadership –
in order to give this powerful and timely knowledge credibility.
I acknowledge that I am a guardian of this message,
but I cannot claim ownership of it.
It has chosen in me a conduit or vehicle,
and it belongs to every one of us: to all humanity, to every human
being.
The Truth was written from a place of unknowing, rather than a
place of knowing:
I learned what is written as it wrote me.
It has transformed my life.

And since reading it, I've discovered it aligns with the greatest

spiritual teachings of all time.

I feel deeply privileged, blessed and a little daunted

to be the initial bearer of such an original, and transformative new

way of being.

I thank you genuinely in advance,

from the bottom of my soul,

and on behalf of the soul of us all,

for spreading the word

to enable

the Truth to do its work:

creating the transformative seeing, doing and being we all so

desperately seek and need

to birth a new world.

Yours, as One with you, and with the deepest love,

AD Infinitum

I am by no means perfect,
I'm part of the collateral damage,
just like everyone else.

Introduction

The way you perceive your Self is what enables, or disables, you.

In our current Western culture we function as part of an established system. However, without awareness, many of us lose our Selves in this system. We become diminished and mechanized by it. We lose our Essence, our vitality, and even our innate sense of being or humanity. This defeats and disables us.

We can feel like we're going around and around, in circles, like a moth mesmerized by a bright light. And believe it or not, this is not how it's supposed to be. For society to flourish we are supposed to feel exhausted, overwhelmed, isolated and unfulfilled. You see, when we feel unfulfilled, too exhausted and overwhelmed to know what we really need, we become susceptible to what we are told we need. And corporate society pumps us with what *feeds it*: it tells us constantly that we need to produce, spend, and aspire to all that keeps us unfulfilled. That way, we become life-long "consumers" who feed the system and starve our vitality.

The more connected to soul-less pursuits we are, the more lost we are. And as a human race we have never been more lost than we are today.

So many of us know this. Millions of us are searching. We know, deep down, that even many of the greatest religions have been corrupted by the theme of today – the corporate mindset and the soul-less agenda. We are searching for more. And this search is the most vital of all – for every one of us, at both an individual and collective level.

The simple fact is we have lost our True Selves in the habit of our existence. And the reason is very simple: we have forgotten who we really are. That's why The Truth is here. It awakens who we are. It enables us to rediscover our astoundingly powerful essence and our interconnected wholeness. It allows us complete fulfillment. We receive the rudder we need to live the life we were designed to live: the elemental message at the basis of all uncorrupted religion. This is the fundamental knowing that every great master or teacher tried to help us learn. We unveil The Truth that lies hidden in all our indigenous history. And we finally discover the tools we need to set our Selves free, regardless of culture, faith, race or creed.

Congratulations on being part of The Truth Revolution. Thank you for being in tune enough to find it. As you read this message know you are making history!

All religions of the world, while they may differ in other respects,
unitedly proclaim that nothing lives in this world but truth.
Mahatma Gandhi

Part One:

Welcome to the Revelation

Starting Thoughts

Once you realize you can tap into the Energy of ALL life,
you will be able to connect to the greatest power of all.
You will enable unthinkable magnificence in your life
and the world around you.

This book is your road map to a revolutionary way of thinking, and
being.
It is what each one of us seeks, whether we know it or not.

I offer you peace.
I offer you love.
I offer you friendship.
I see your beauty.
I hear your need.
I feel your feelings.
My wisdom flows from the highest source.
I salute that source in you.
Let us work together in unity and love.

Mohandas (Mahatma) Gandhi

1.0

Part One

Who Do You Think You Are?

Think of this as the cocoon phase of your metamorphosis. You are going into a deep place of self-discovery, which will provide you a passage through to your transformed Self.

So let's begin with you, and your perception of you.

How would you describe yourself? You may begin with your name, age, gender, race, culture, religion, and perhaps a bit of your history. Then you may include some of your talents or abilities. You may include your socio-economic status, education or social standing. Then you could mention some of your personality traits, likes or dislikes. And you may add in your current family circumstances. The end result may sound something like this: I'm David Smith, thirty-two-years-old, a male Caucasian of Irish decent. I'm a middle-class, private-school educated lawyer and although I grew up in a Catholic family, I now consider myself an atheist. I'm a perfectionist, a bit of a control freak and extremely competitive. And it's these things, I believe, that have made me successful in life. I'm a great golfer, am fit and like to eat well. I love animals and have three dogs, although I struggle with close human relationships. I also have a four-year-old daughter, although I've never been married. I'm rather commitment phobic.

Well the truth is 'David Smith' is *none* of what he describes. Everything he referred to simply reflects the *connections* he has made in his life. These connections have affected what he has done with his life, the choices he has made, and where he has landed up, but they are not him. He is beyond all of that.

Before we go into who David really is, and who we really are, we first need to look at the *Power of Connection*.

The ultimate value of life depends upon awareness and the power of contemplation rather than upon mere survival.
Aristotle

1.1

The Power of Connection

Essentially, when you are born, becoming a physical part of this world, you came about through an extensive series of connections.

Starting with a sperm and an egg, each cell in your body grew out of, and through, a connection to already existing cells, or life. An automatic, spontaneous series of connections occurred, and through this process you grew your embodied form – from your mother's cells.

Protected in the cocoon of your mother's womb, essentially *Empty Space* and connection enabled the creation of your current perceived existence.

The same process continued to grow you once you took your first breath, connecting you to the air you now breathe second by second. You breathe in *Empty Space*, or air, and then it breathes you. You take in nutrients, or 'food', which is essentially life, and it provides you with life. A significant portion of your body consists of water, and you need to keep taking more of this part of yourself in, in order for your body to survive. Water is life. It is living energy. And as you drink, as it flows through you, you flow and grow through it – and the life it holds.

What this means is you exist purely through a process of continual connection to life around you.

This applies practically, to your living body and being. It also applies psychologically, spiritually and mentally as your personal connections to people, environments and experiences feed, fuel, mold and develop you.

There are only two mistakes one can make along the road to truth:
Not going all the way, and not starting.
Buddha

1.1.1   Imposed Connections

As a baby and young child, your experiences and just about everything you learned were imposed upon you. You learned what your parents or guardians, and the world you were exposed to, taught you. Your experiences shaped you, but you *did not choose* or determine them.

In all likelihood, you will have 'learned' things like: how you fit into the world, your personal value, what differentiates you, how safe the surroundings are, whether people are good, kind and dependable or not, what love is and how to express it, how you should behave, what matters most, and how people of your gender, race, religion, culture, social standing and economic status *should* think, feel and act. As a result, you would have formed a strong self-perception by the time you reached the age of about eight: the age considered to be the 'age of reason'.

This self-perception would have been formed through all your connections to date, none of which you would have chosen. So we can call these early and very formative connections *Imposed Connections.*

From here, you would have used your self-perception, based on your *Imposed Connections*, to make more connections. These *Imposed Connections* would have affected how you thought about others, yourself and challenges. They would have influenced your reactions to situations, people and life in general. Your *Imposed Connections* would have determined your focus, and your focus would have determined your future connections. So around and around it goes, and it grows you.

Unfortunately, the problem with *Imposed Connections* is we are usually oblivious to them. Worse still, they are formed before we are able to maturely assess them – often before the age of reason. And then they reign over us, somewhat like a compass or rudder, directing and distracting us. So *Imposed Connections* have the capacity to block our joy and passions – and even hijack our life.

For instance, a four-year-old child who playfully picks up a knife and sticks it in a power point may have received a painful slap across the ear followed by an angry, "You stupid idiot!" from his father. From then on, he could have perhaps felt scared of his Dad, stupid, and even unloved. He may have, unknowingly, spent most of his life living up to that immature perceived sense-making: behaving stupidly, scared and unlovable. Or he may have focused all his energy on trying to disprove this assumed interpretation: trying extra hard to be smart, brave and lovable. Either way, his entire life would obliviously be *reflecting* an irrational connection he made when he was four.

Tragically, his father was actually reflecting (be it rather clumsily) his love for his son and the fear of losing him; basically the opposite of what the boy connected to.

This boy could then even go on to later become an electrician, driven by an unconscious desire to illogically rectify this defining moment in his life. It's incredible that when you ask people what their most powerful first memory is; it regularly corresponds to what they do with their life. The woman who helps violent men rehabilitate had an abusive father. The family law solicitor or policeman faced serious injustice as a child. The nurse had a sick family member or strong hospital memories. The famous entertainer felt unnoticed, alone or unloved as a child. And the electrician was belted at four when he played with the fuse box.

You see, connections can be made to things or feelings that don't even exist. Then they can form and create us, subconsciously. We unknowingly seek to fill the gap.

Perhaps you could take a moment to examine some of your *Imposed Connections*.

Consider the socio-economic, cultural, political, social landscape you were born into. What were the struggles of the time? What were your greatest personal challenges, how did you overcome them and how did those around you react? How were you supported by those around you? Describe your parents/guardians most prevalent belief systems. Were children valued and listened to; expected to be seen and not heard, or something else? How loving, nurturing and responsive was the environment in which you were raised? What difficulties did your parents face and how did they affect you? What rules or expectations were imposed? Were you punished and if so how? How did this make you feel? What kind of family and social examples were set? How was conflict resolved? Consider the dominant themes and the popular views of the time. What about the influence of media – what were you exposed to in terms of movies, games, music, media or websites?

These kinds of memories can be difficult to access, especially when considering your early years, as important incidents often occur before recall ability has been formed at around two years of age. Also memories fade or are distorted by what is later said to have happened. Therefore, the most accurate memories can often be found in your feelings: ask yourself how you *felt* as a child.

Consider how you felt about yourself, your family members, your teachers, your community and the world at large. Don't worry if there's not much there yet. It will come.

Then try to remember your strongest childhood memory. Does it in correspond to what you do with your life? Could it have started an underlying rationale in your life – subliminally? Try to recall how you *felt* at the time of this memory and what you made it mean to you. What did you decide – about yourself, perhaps about others or even the world – based on this incident? Now think of a child, not you, and consider what you would tell them if you had the opportunity to hear their immature sense making.

It's interesting how Imposed Connections can commandeer us, unconsciously. We can make virtually unmemorable connections, and play them out unknowingly for the rest of our lives.

Worse still, usually our strongest childhood memories are traumatic, so commonly people form their entire life direction based on the one-out-of-a-hundred distressing event. So, if you're a plumber who has an early unpleasant memory relating to a toilet, sink or water pipe, you may have established your first clue as to why your job has never felt satisfying – but rather like something you feel you ought to do.

We are what we repeatedly do*.
Aristotle

---

*Aristotle was perhaps saying we become what we repeatedly do.
This is who we begin being.

1.1.2   Foundational Connections

It is now a well-established fact, according to world leaders in the area of early childhood development, that the first two to eight years of our life are the "formative years" (please see Notes at the end of this Chapter). The first six months are considered to be the most formative, the first two years the next most formative and so on until we are around eight years of age – at which point our underlying personality is believed to have been fully formed.

We now know that our brain development is permanently altered, and our "emotional memory" constructed, through our early childhood experiences: our early *Imposed Connections*. This is despite the fact that often our most fundamental emotional responses are to events we cannot consciously recall because they happened before the age of eighteen months when recall ability was not yet developed (Mate, G., 2010). For this reason, just as a fish in polluted water will perish or a plant in barren soil will wither, a neglected baby cannot flourish.

These early years could also be called the imprint years because what happens to us then stays with us for life like a permanent stamp and hidden helmsman.

We then continue to react to our environment, as we are still forming, but based on what is formed already. We begin to make our own decisions and choices and we decide what we connect to – based on what we have *already decided* life means. And what we have decided life means depends on our *Imposed Connections*.

So what appears to be our free choice is actually a reflection of an interpretation of our *Imposed Connections*. The big 'choices' we make about what is fundamentally right or wrong, acceptable or unacceptable, are all based on what we received in our Foundational years. They can therefore be called *Foundational Connections*.

What this means is we continue to make connections that form us, direct us, enable or disable us, based on subconscious connections we made before we could walk or talk.

For example, your Grandmother may be a wonderful nurturer. This may be something she gifts the world. If you look back far enough, though, you will undoubtedly find a very good reason for her comforting nature. It can almost be guaranteed that her formative years held great nurturing experiences, *or* the complete opposite. You see, she will either be repeating her *Imposed Connections*, or correcting them. 'Nurturing' became a direction she took for the rest of her life, based on her un-chosen Imposed start to life. So 'nurturing' became one of her *Foundational Connections*. This is what we all do, without awareness.

Our Foundational Connections reflect our fundamental choices and views, our underlying belief system and values. They directly correspond to what was Imposed upon us.

All forms of judgment and hostility, including racism, sexism, and other forms of oppression, reflect *Foundational Connections*. They reflect our ingrained programming, *not* who we are.

Often wars are started over *Foundational Connections* – and not just on a global scale, but also between husbands and wives, or neighbors and community members.

You may, for example, land yourself with two kids and a partner who constantly seems unsupportive. You could spend years and hundreds of dollars on counseling, only to realise the entire problem between you comes from your *Foundational Connection* to the principle: "marriage equals equality". Your partner may have a completely different *Foundational Connection* – perhaps: "the man is the head of the house". Until you both understand where the contradiction is coming from, it's unlikely you will ever find a real resolution.

Additionally problematic is we often assume that the people we are most compatible with, or close to, share the same *Foundational Connections* as us. This frequently leads to disappointment or conflict. In fact, the strongest relationships often face these value-style clashes, and that is why love sometimes turns into hatred.

Siblings can argue over different individual interpretations of the same *Imposed Connections*. They can play out opposite responses to the same start to life. For example, one may form *Foundational Connections* that repeat a cycle of aggression, or manipulation, while the other may shun away from that completely becoming extremely gentle and honest. Obvious clashes would then arise.

We see these clashes regularly between parents and children, as parents assume their kids should share *their* own *Foundational Connections*. This is not only unreasonable but impossible because we are all individuals with unique life experiences, and a distinct interpretation of them. Additionally, as the example above demonstrates, we commonly form *Foundational Connections* that directly oppose what we were exposed to. For instance, if we were hit as children we could smack our own children – or we could passionately disapprove of any form of violence against children. Therefore, our *Foundational Connections* could conflict with our parents' completely. And that can cause great contention.

Knowing this is liberating.

For example, if a son reveals the fact that he is gay and his father orders him out of the house, he would feel deeply wounded and abandoned. However, if he understood that his father's *Foundational Connections*, which may for instance stem from his *Imposed Connections* of a deeply entrenched religious indoctrination, he would know that his Dad is not able to make a 'free choice'. He is instead automatically responding to a

THE TRUTH AD INFINITUM

subconscious pre-programming that he has no awareness or control over.

Understanding this, the son would be able to see his father as being caught in a trap. Then, instead of fueling the anger and ignorance with more anger and ignorance, the son would be able to understand his Dad's *predictable* reaction compassionately. The whole situation becomes a lot less personal.

This is why we often see remarkable patterns repeated. Is it a coincidence that so many of us become either just like our parents, or the exact opposite? I would suggest not. We are reflecting our connections to our past – either through avoiding them or replaying them. When we do either without awareness, we are allowing our connections to control us rather than being in control of them. And what this means is we have lost who we really are.

The significant problems we face in life cannot be solved
at the same level of thinking we were at when we created them.
Albert Einstein

1.2

Finding Freedom

When we lose who we really are, we feel lost.

No matter how hard we try, to feel fulfilled, to feel less empty, to feel less lost, it simply cannot work when we have lost our Selves.

When we think we are our *Foundational Connections*, and we allow *Imposed Connections* to steer us, and define us, subconsciously, we abandon our True Self. We lose our *essence*. And we lose what is *essence*-ial to our purpose, meaning and vitality. We become trapped in Connections that govern us, without our knowing. Some may be Destructive to us, and others Constructive, but we have no discernment because we are completely oblivious to what is driving us – and to who we *really* are.

The great news is this trap is completely reversible. Freedom awaits you. And it's much simpler than you may think. All that's required is awareness. Once you recognize the Truth, your perception of your Self, and every living being, will alter. Instantly. And you will be set free. Automatically.

Consider for a moment, Bobo, a circus elephant. No one could believe it when they saw Bobo standing in the middle of a park, with no fence or restraint. He just stood there, swaying and treading grass. People wondered why he didn't wander off – or even wander around. What an amazing elephant! Well Bobo had been chained, with a very short three-foot chain, to a post – for the first few years of his life. These were his formative years. Then later, his shackles were removed. But Bobo stood, every day, in the same spot, still confined to the tiny single square meter of ground around him. His previously enforced boundaries forever enslaved him, despite the reality of his freedom. People would pass by, inspired by what appeared to be a willing circus participant; but the only reason Bobo complied was because of his *perceived* restraint. His *Imposed Connections* had been removed, but were so deeply entrenched they had formed *Foundational Connections*, which trapped him – even when the *Imposed Connections* were no longer there. This powerful, majestic and magnificent animal had no recognition of the fact that he was, in reality, the largest mammal on earth, capable of enduring life through the harshest of conditions. Bobo had lost sight of who he was. His perceptions had robbed him of his Essence. His immense strength would never be discovered. He lived, forever a shadow of his True Self.

Without awareness, every one of us is at risk of living trapped, an unfulfilled trace of our Self, by our own sense of who we are.

Our 'chains' are our *Imposed* and *Foundational Connections* – but only when we believe they define who we are, and what we can be.

Imagine if Bobo was able to comprehend that although he was chained for the first few years of his life, those chains do not determine his boundaries. He would then be free as soon as the chains were removed, right? But the problem Bobo had is no one had told him, or shown him who he was. So he had no way of knowing. Therefore even if he were able to realize his freedom, he wouldn't know what to do with it. He wouldn't know *how* to *be* an elephant and how to do what fulfills elephants.

In this same way, we are shackled by our Imposed perception of our Self. We are limited and bound by it. We have lost our Selves in it. And the only way to our freedom is to uncover who we really are.

Do not conform any longer to the pattern of this world,
but be transformed by the renewing of your mind.
Romans 12:2 NIV

1.2.1   Who Are You Really?

So who are you then, if you are none of what you've thought you were for your entire life? Who is 'David Smith' if he is none of what he describes himself as at the beginning of this Chapter? If these things keep him trapped and limited, what is he trapped and limited from being? If they don't define him, then what does?

Well, here's the thing:

YOU are anything and everything, unlimited I'm possibility, infinite and boundless, the Essence of ALL life.

That may sound a little extreme to you at the moment. If so, that's understandable. It would be like Bobo trying to comprehend who he really was after half a lifetime in self-perception confinement. He would understandably struggle to comprehend The Truth. Well, you could be equally trapped – *and* if you are, you are equally a simple shift in consciousness away from your freedom.

But what does freedom mean, you may ask. What does it mean to me, to my life? How can I *be* this infinite boundless Energy of *I'm possibility*? Well that's what The Truth is here to help you do. Our entire journey together will unfold your new way of being. But first you must understand who you really are.

See if you can resist the temptation to decide what it all means, for now. Simply read on. Listen with your heart, and your SOUL, to the message, and let it sit quietly within you. Allow it to resonate. Notice how it *feels* – how you feel. What it means and how it frees you will evolve, one step at a time, just as you do. It will happen with perfect precision and it will occur automatically, subliminally and effortlessly. All you need do right now is *just trust* the process and your deepest inner knowing.

Make the connection consciously, and the cells of your body will change you subconsciously.

So now we will look at the vital elements that make up who you really are.

And the point is, to live everything.
Live the questions now.
Perhaps you will then gradually, without noticing it,
live along some distant day into the answer.
Rainer Maria Rilke

1.2.2 Empty Space

At the beginning of this Chapter we discussed connection and the fact that you exist entirely through a process of connection. We also remembered that your life began in the perceived *Empty Space* of your mother's womb (1.1).

We discussed the fact that as you read these pages you take in air, and that air breathes you into being, second by second. That air is also often perceived as *Empty Space*.

Now before you were born, what were you? Where were you? At what point did you begin to exist? Was it at the time of conception? Well if it was, then where were you a moment before conception?

Were you in a perceived *Empty Space* perhaps, before you even existed? If you were, what were you? Were you part of this *Empty Space*? And isn't *Empty Space* no-thing? One thing we can be certain of is out of this un-definable *Empty Space* of no-thing came everything you are.

Michael Talbot, the late esteemed Quantum Physicist and revolutionary thinker, explains how through extensive scientific research, it has been *proven* that *Empty Space* is not empty. It is in fact full. As he states, "is a plenum as opposed to a vacuum, and is the ground of existence of everything, including ourselves" (please see Notes at the end of this Chapter).

Talbot asserts that all of space is awash with waves that contain energy, and that each cubic meter of empty space contains more energy than the total energy of all matter in the known universe!

Is it then possible that you are, elementally, this plenum? Could you, at a Core level, be pure vitality and Energy – the Energy of all possibility, of life itself? Surely if you came from *Empty Space*, you grew out of it, and you take it in each moment of your existence in order to exist, it could actually be at least part of your form. And if *Empty Space*, or no-thing, is actually the Energy of every-thing, then you are actually fundamentally part of every-thing. And there is actually no limit to what you can be, do or create.

Sound phenomenal? Well you are!

Nothing exists except atoms and empty space;
Everything else is an opinion.
Democritus

1.2.3   Life-Generating Energy

If you are, elementally, part of this Energy of all existence, then you must be part of the Essence of existence.

And if all existence comes from this Energy, then you must be intrinsically connected to and interconnected with all life – past, present and future. You share your Source of existence with all other existence and you are ultimately part of *all* other living Energy.

Finally, if you are – at least at a root level – part of the Energy of all life, you must also be fundamentally *Life-Generating Energy*. Because what else can the Energy of all life be but *Life-Generating*?

Now think about water again for a moment. You probably know that your physical body is made up of around 60% water. And in order to survive you need to constantly give your body more of what it at least partially *is* – water. In fact, without water you would struggle to live much longer than two or three days.

And think about air – or *Empty Space*. How long do you think you could live without that? Well, is this not also because you need to 'feed' your Self with what you fundamentally are?

So if you essentially are *Life-Generating Energy*, then in order to thrive, it makes sense that you will need to 'feed' your Self, or surround your Self, with as much *Life-Generating Energy* as you can. Make sense?

There is only one breath.
All are made of the same clay.
The light within all is the same.
Guru Granth Sahib

1.2.4   Source Energy

Every living creature or organism is alive because of one reason only: it possesses living energy. Living energy is life. Without it, we would cease to be alive. In fact, even non-living forms hold living energy: they carry the energy of life around them.

Energy generates life, using connection as a process. But where does *Life-Generating Energy* come from? Let's go back to your conception again. What generated your initial connection, sparking the beginning of your life? How did that sperm know where to go and what to do? Who was directing it? Was the sperm already an aware living entity, with its own mind and sense of direction, or was it directed? If it was directed, what directed it? How did the egg know what to do when the sperm came along? What made them, now connected, move to the perceived *Empty Space* of the womb? Did they have consciousness yet? Did they know they were about to grow this tiny "seed" into your life? What *made* your seed grow? What makes any seed grow? How does a flower know how to blossom? How does the sun know how to rise? How does a consciousness occur in a fully-fledged human being as result of a woman's egg and a man's sperm?

These questions, and many more like them, are the timeless and unanswerable questions we will forever ask. We will never have a definitive answer although many religions will profess to offer one.

Unfortunately, our quest for answers may be jeopardizing our ability to be who we are. Every time we claim to have an answer, we are losing potentially vital possibilities.

With every claimed answer we are shutting off the vitality that comes with living the questions.

There will never be scientific proof. We may never *know* the answers, yet we may develop a sense or *feel* of them through living the questions. We will never find a puppeteer behind the scenes of every living moment whom we can capture and cage, examine and decipher. These mysteries will remain until the end of time.

In saying this, there is one thing we know for sure. We know there is something beyond us generating life in a way we could never even comprehend. We don't need to get caught up in religion (although we can); we simply need to acknowledge this vital fact.

For the sake of simplicity, lets call this mysterious and unfathomable life force *Source Energy*. This seems like a sensible name, would you not agree, since it is the ultimate life energy behind, before and within all life?

So *Source Energy* makes life happen, magically or mind-bogglingly. Could you consider it possible then that this same energy can bring your life into contact with another's to create magnificent growth? This energy brought the egg and sperm together – two previously separate living entities that had no conception of one another until they came together to create your conception. Could it not then also create and generate other incredible *Life-Generating Connections*? If so, how could you help enable and encourage the process?

Would it make sense that to enable and encourage the process, you could connect to it – this *Source Energy*? As a matter of fact, arguably you came from this *Source Energy* in the first place, did you not? And doesn't that mean that you are innately part of it, connected to it in the most profound way?

The fabled musk deer searches the world over for the source of the scent which comes from itself.
Ramakrishna

So, we already know that in order to thrive, we need to feed our Selves with what we already are. Then it makes sense that if we connect to *Source Energy*, we are automatically connecting to the

Essence of our existence and of all life. Surely nothing could be more powerful and enriching?

Is it possible that this *Source Energy* could therefore be the most powerful connection we can make?

How then do we connect to *Source Energy*? Well, once we know what it is, it's very easy. In fact it's probably the most natural connection we can make.

You see, *Source Energy* is the *Life-Generating Energy* that lies at the Source of all life and existence. We already know that life comes about through the *Empty Space* of no-thing. So *Source Energy* can be found in no-thing: that place of silence, the moments *between* your breath. *Source Energy* can be found in the *Empty Space* of the air you breathe, so by focusing on your breath, and allowing your Self to *feel* the moments between your breaths, you are connecting to *Source Energy*. *Source Energy* lies at the heart of nature: you can feel it as it floats you its salty waters, you can hear it in the song of a skylark or the roar of thunder, you can taste it in the flesh of a peach or the juice of an orange, you can smell it in the scent of the eucalyptus tree or a rose. All you need to do is stop: and listen, taste, smell, see, hear and feel. Connect to life around you, and allow it to flow through you. You can call this *Sense-you-all* Living: *sense* that *you* are part of *all* life.

Source Energy is everywhere, and you can connect to it in the moment-to-moment successions of life: the moment-to-moment changes in the tide, or the wind; the moment-to-moment reshaping of the clouds or the stars; the moment-to-moment flicker of a fire or a candle light; the moment-to-moment exchange of air and life as you become mesmerized by the miracle of your own existence. All you need do is *notice*, and *focus* – on life, second by second, minute by minute. You can think of this also as *Succession-all Living*. And it enables Success-in-all Life.

You can 'speak' to *Source Energy*. And you don't need to do it out loud. It doesn't matter whether you call this Source Energy Greater Energy, The Universe, God, or any other title. Neither does it matter whether you call what you are doing prayer, meditation, connection or anything else. What matters is that you make the connection. Then you will plug your Self In to the power Source of all life. Listen to your deepest feelings. Be guided by your intuition, your inner knowing, for this is the voice of Source Energy, driving you to I'm-possibility. Resist the temptation to make sense of it all. Then *just trust*. Let it be. Flow with life, and allow life to flow with and through you. Don't be surprised though, when you do these things regularly, your life will change remarkably. It will feel like you've replaced your AA batteries with electricity. This is the most powerful connection in the universe.

Self-realization means that we have been consciously   connected with our source of
being.
Once we have made   this connection, then nothing can go wrong.
Swami Paramananda

1.2.5   Love

What is Love?

"Love" has been tossed around almost slanderously, in agenda-driven campaigns, from politics, advertising and movies, to dysfunctional relationships. It has therefore unfortunately lost much of its meaning. In fact, many of us will admit to not really knowing what it means or how to describe it. We feel it, but what is it? All we do know is it's something magnificent that cannot really be defined – a bit like us ourselves, huh?

The Truth is Love is all that is Life-Generating. Anything else is not Love.

Source Energy is the Source of all life, making it the ultimate Life-Generating force. So Source Energy is Pure Love.

And you came from Source Energy, which is Pure Love, so you too are inherently Pure Love.

Your task is not to seek for love,
But merely to seek
And find all the barriers
Within yourself
That you have
Built against it.
Rumi

What this means is the more Pure Love you connect to, and the more you act and be from the Core of your being, which is Pure Love, the more authentic you will be. You will be who you were born to be. And you will be feeding your Self with the most fulfilling and nourishing 'food' available to you.

Love

Love what is in

deep within

You

And every one

of you.

Love

All.

And then you

will know

Love.

Then you will know

Your Self.

It is unlikely a coincidence that those who have spent their entire lives researching what we require elementally to be fulfilled and happy, generally agree that once our basic physiological requirements are met – such as food, water, shelter and sleep – we all need to feel secure and connected deeply to others through meaning and *love* (Abraham Maslow's Hierarchy of Needs provides a famous example). This is how we thrive as opposed to simply survive. Love provides us with a meaningful and worthwhile sense of purpose. It gives us what we most need in order to live a fulfilled life.

Victor Frankl, a leading neurologist, psychiatrist and Holocaust survivor, was awarded twenty-nine honorary degrees for his contribution to individual freedom. He attributed "meaning in life" and "something to live for" – or some*one* to live for – as our driving motivational life force. He believed that without a love-directed sense of purpose, we wither, losing survival incentive. What this means is our primary need is to belong, to love and to be loved.

46

Concentration camps provided evidence of this fact – with those who had someone or something they loved deeply and wanted to live for, surviving those who did not. Then after the war, Frankl discovered mundane and meaningless everyday lives, directed in loveless ways, resulted in depression and a reduced desire to live.

The truth –
that love is the ultimate and the highest goal to which man can aspire.
Victor Frankl

So a lack of Love – loving others, being loved, and coming from a place of love – makes us un-loved. And if, elementally, *we are Love*, then we feel 'un-our Self'. We feel lost. And we call it feeling un-well. We wither like the plant in nutrient deprived soil, because we are starving our Selves of what we most need to thrive.

1.2.6   One

If all life comes from the one Source, and every living being is interconnected at an organic root level, then it follows that we are all essentially ONE.

We are one, after all, you and I.
Together we suffer, together we exist and forever will recreate each other.
Pierre Teilhard de Chardin

We are like cells in a body. We are separate, individual parts of the same body of existence. We, as humanity, form a greater power, and all add up and work together to function and keep the greater body we all live and exist in alive. We are indwelling and inter-dwelling, despite our perceived separateness.

You may have heard of the term "butterfly effect", made popular by the movie of the same title. The late mathematician, meteorologist and pioneering Chaos Theorist, Edward Lorenz, coined the term. It questioned whether the flap of a butterfly's wings in Brazil could set off a tornado in Texas. And it was determined mathematically, that every tiny part of anything affects everything. It's not a romantic illusion, but a scientific fact.

For this reason, each action, thought and feeling you live is a small mirror, or *reflection*, of your larger self.

And, by the same token, each action, thought and feeling we each live affects every one of us.

We are not as separate as we think.

There's a name for this in Chaos Theory also: "fractals". The idea is you can look at a drop of water to understand the sea (Kuhn, L., 2009). Well, in this same way, you can look at one thought, one feeling or one action in yourself, to understand your 'me'. And you can look at one person to understand our 'we'.

You can learn a lot about something massive by looking at a minute part of it. Likewise, small actions can create and generate great and unexpected change – in any-thing, any-one, and every-thing.

Michael Talbot explains how when a holographic rose is cut in half, each half will contain within it the entire whole. He asks us to consider the fact that, similarly, for example, when an embryo is divided, we don't get half a baby – instead we get twins. He suggests that this, and countless other forces of nature, prove a commonality between our existence and holograms. Within each whole are an infinite number of smaller wholes.

Perhaps our perceived separateness is keeping us divided, dismantled and lost.

Although still groundbreaking, these findings are attracting the attention of scientists worldwide. Basil Hiley, a physicist at Birbeck College, London, informs us after examining these findings:

We must be prepared to consider radically new views of reality.
Basil Hiley

Not that we need an explanation, but this theory would explain how within what appears to be no-thing is every-thing. It, and the fact that we are innately interconnected, further demystifies, at least to a certain extent, paranormal phenomenon as well as miraculous healing and synchronicity. It proves that at an elemental level we are all smaller parts of one larger whole.

Our body itself provides evidence of this life property. Iridology, reflexology and acupuncture, for example, rely on the understanding that tiny points on our body can be interpreted or manipulated to repair or affect our greater body. A pinpoint on our foot, for instance, stimulated appropriately, can help restore the whole of our liver. These traditional healing arts are becoming increasingly popular as their successes often outweigh that of Western medicine.

On an individual level, we can 'fix' large parts of our Self through small changes. And as you will discover we, at a greater life level, even at a humanitarian or planetary level, can rehabilitate, reinvigorate, regenerate and rebuild what we all need most, through small triggers that result in great impact.

Think of this wise saying: What's the difference between Wellness and Illness? *WE*llness involves *WE*, and *I*llness involves *I*.

1.2.7   Interconnected Web

Esteemed Quantum Physicist, Bohm was mind-blown by Alain Aspect and his teams' potentially revolutionary discovery in 1982, at the University of Paris. Aspect found that subatomic particles, such as electrons, communicate with one another, instantaneously. The distance between these particles made no difference – they could be a few feet apart or ten billion miles away from one another. These findings bring Einstein's theory that communication can never travel faster than the speed of light into question. They also provide scientific evidence confirming the fact that we are all interconnected (please see Notes at the end of this Chapter).

Bohm describes our universe akin to a kind of giant superhologram, whereby our objective reality can be affected or even created by what we put into it. This means that every thought you have, and every thing you do affects everyone and everything.

As our human bodies are made up of protons, neurons and electrons – in the form of atoms – then it makes sense that cells in our brain, for example, could communicate instantly, and simultaneously, with cells in our liver, or leg for arguments sake. It also suggests that cells in *my* heart could connect or communicate instantly and simultaneously with cells in *your* brain and your heart. In fact, *our* cells could instantly and simultaneously connect to and communicate with subatomic particles that comprise each star lighting the night's sky, each fish decorating the seabed, and each leaf oxygenating the air.

It's even possible and perhaps likely when applying this theory, that these kinds of connections and communications are happening all the time – but we are simply not allowing our Selves to 'see' them, perceive them, connect to them, or be attuned to them: we are unable to *feel* them, sense them and *be* consciously part of them. So, we are unable to interpret and compute these connections, despite the fact that they exist. In the same way that billions of people starve or suffer every day in our world (even in houses or suburbs next door), while others live a comfortable existence; we live our lives disconnected to all kinds of realities. However, the realities still exist. We simply don't see them, so we don't take them in, and they hence are not part of our reality – even though they are in fact our (greater) reality.

We are part of, and connected to, all we know and everything we don't know, whether we know it or not.

To see the World in a Grain of Sand
And a heaven in a Wild Flower,
Hold Infinity in the palm of your hand
And Eternity in an hour.
William Blake

Once we accept we are inherently and indelibly interconnected, we will open pathways that will take us to brilliant, currently inconceivable, destinations.

1.3

What it all Means

What it all means is the labels and definitions we give our Selves do not define us; they confine us. Just as the baby elephant is eluded by early Imposed boundaries that no longer exist, any superficial definitions of our Selves keeps us equally trapped and diminished – through sheer false perception.

If you were fortunate enough to grow up with reliable, loving, nurturing and responsive care, the *Imposed Connections* they provided would have nourished you. You will be much more likely to naturally, automatically develop *Foundational Connections* that grow and enable you positively. You will be more likely to forge healthy relationships and connections.

However, if you were isolated, emotionally abandoned, betrayed or abused, you, through no fault of your own, could have found yourself subconsciously following a Destructive connection path – *until* such time as you were actually able to *see* what you are unknowingly doing.

And even those who believe they had the perfect formative years will have gathered *Imposed Connections*, which will have affected their *Foundational Connections*, for both better and worse. The point is once we know what has been forming us up until now, we can choose to be re-formed, instantly. And it will happen automatically. All that's required is a change in perception, awareness and consciousness.

Mind is consciousness which has put on limitations.
You are originally unlimited and perfect.
Later you take on limitations and become the mind.
Ramana Maharshi

There's a complex term known as "autopoiesis" in Chaos and Complexity Theory, used to describe the self-generating, automatic and continuous process of life and survival (please see Notes at the end of this Chapter). But you don't need complicated words to understand that magically, miraculously, every millisecond; your heart beats, your blood pumps and your organs continue to thankfully automatically repeat patterns, self-generate and adapt in order to keep the organism that is *you* alive. Not only do you do this, but you also automatically evolve to suit your ever-changing environment.

To put it overly simply, the point of this entire book is about re-awakening your Self, and re-mind-ing you how to naturally evolve, *flow,* flourish and grow, magically, miraculously and magnificently, with and through the process of life itself. This is the ultimate human journey. It is why we are all here. And it provides us with the knowing and sense of belonging we all long for.

So, first and foremost, begin here by celebrating the miracle you are! Every second that you are alive is living proof of how energy and connection work magically in action.

Then realize you are none of what you thought you were. You have never been what you were told you are.

What you are is Unlimited Free Life-Generating Energy. You are embodied Love. And you are interconnected in the most profound and powerful way to the Source of all life, and to every living being.

Step-by-step, as you read ahead, you will discover how to apply this knowing to your day-to-day life. Your life will transform automatically and transcend your greatest dreams. You will find ways to apply this breakthrough practically. The theory will completely alter your grounded reality. You will uncover the patterns that keep you entrenched in diminishing dogma and lost. You will break these old habits, easily. You will see the light and begin living your Truth. What may feel like an epiphany now will seem like the most familiar thing you've ever known. Just let it happen.   Trust.   This   process   will   unfold   you,   subliminally.   You

need do *no-thing*.

---

*For hundreds of years our worldview has been shaped by a scientific story
describing isolated beings competing for survival on a lonely planet in an
indifferent universe.
...I intend to explore the enormous implications of the
new scientific story unfolding,
which shows that at the subatomic level, we are not alone, but are part of a vast
quantum web of connection and evolution.
To be true to ourselves and our most fundamental nature, we must remake our
world anew.
Lynne McTaggart*

Author's Note

Take Time to Gather Your Self

If you're like most of us,
you may feel like your head is spinning.
You could even be feeling a little disorientated right now.

I know when I received this new insight or learning,
it took a good few weeks to 'digest'.
As I digested it, I noticed my life changing.
My thoughts automatically altered,
virtually subconsciously,
adjusting my connections
rather effortlessly.
My life began to change
quite unbelievably.
I noticed more 'coincidences' occurring;
more 'magic'.
I simply felt like I was beginning to flow with life,
rather than fight it.

I invite you to take a break
for a day or two,
or a few days,
from reading at this point.
A 'break' now will not be a waste of time,
but rather a part of your passage through.

Often breaks allow break-throughs.
You may not notice questions arising
as you engage in living the learning,
but they will.
And then the answers will have more meaning
and relevance
when you discover them.

See if you can just live life
and notice what is different.
You don't need to do anything.

THE TRUTH AD INFINITUM

Remember, this is a pilgrimage.
It's a walk into a changed tomorrow.
You are forging a new path,
one that was not there yesterday.
What matters is not how quickly you take this knowing in,
but how profoundly.

The next chapter settles you in to this knowing.
It takes on a new pace,
and again shifts gear.
It drums in the reality of what you have taken in,
applying it practically
in a deeply grounded way.

Thank you for sharing this remarkable trip
into unimaginable new beginnings.
Yours eternally,

AD Infinitum

The words of Rumi

If ten lamps are in one place,
each differs in form from another;
yet you can't distinguish
whose radiance is whose
…when you focus on the light.
In the field of spirit
there is no division;
no individuals exist.
Sweet is the oneness
of the Friend with His Friends.
Catch hold of spirit.
Help the headstrong self disintegrate;
that beneath it you may discover unity,
like a buried treasure.

Everything you see has its roots in the unseen world.
The forms may change,
yet the essence remains the same.
Every wonderful sight will vanish;
every sweet word will fade.
But do not be disheartened.
The source they come from is eternal,
growing, branching out,
giving new life and new joy.
Why do you weep?
The source is within you
and the whole world
is springing up form it.

Jalal Uddin Rumi, 13ᵗʰ Century Sufi Mystic

Notes

Here are just a few experts who provide us with global research and evidence to prove our brains are affected and formed depending on the nurturing we receive or don't receive in our early years: Sue Gerhardt, author and Early Development Researcher; Richard Wilkinson, Professor Emeritus of Social Epidemiology, University of Nottingham; Dr. Gabor Mate, Physician, author, drug addiction researcher, Portland Society.

Michael Talbot focused his entire life on bringing the research of eminent scientists and physicists together in order to understand the nature of existence. He explains predominantly the work of physicist David Bohm, a protégé of Einstein, and neurophysiologist Karl Pribram, an emeritus professor of psychiatry and psychology at Radford and Stanford University and a board-certified neurosurgeon. Both men worked independently, to suggest that reality holds distinctly holographic features.

The term "autopoiesis" was coined by Chilean cyberneticians and bioepistemologiests Humberto Maturana and Francisco Valera: "Greek word that means literally 'self-production' – auto = self, poiesis = production. We observe self-production in all living systems." (Thorpe, R. & Holt, R. (2008) Sage Dictionary of Qualitative Management. Research. Sage Publications).

Part Two

Welcome to the Evolution

Starting Thoughts

The real answers resonate with you.

You know The Truth.

It rests peacefully within your deepest Self,

within your highest level of being.

Only the world you live in has baffled you with bright lights and

distractions.

You have been bombarded with false directives and delusions.

And you've forgotten what matters most...until now.

Now you are re-minded.

You awaken your sleeping giant, your unstoppable power Essence.

Now you remember the answers that lie waiting within you, to set

you free.

Each soul in entering the material experience
does so for the purposes of advancement
towards that awareness of being fully conscious
of the oneness with the Creative Forces.

Edgar Cayce

2.0

Part Two

Knowing and Being Your True Self

You are still in the cocoon phase of your discovery. You are safe here, in the retreat of these words and this incredible Truth. Now you are about to discover the vital tools required to take you into your surrounding world completely transformed. And then your surrounding world will begin to transform with and through you.

You have delved into a deep place of self-discovery, and you now understand what you are not. You have learned how society and both conscious and subliminal influences can brainwash you into believing you are a shadow of your True Self. And you have seen how easily we can all become 'zombie-fied' by the systems we live in. Knowing this sets you well on your way to living a brand new life: as your powerful, liberated Core Self of *I'm possibility.*

Those who have already travelled this journey unanimously feel that the message awakens an inner knowing – a much more natural way of being. And it happens automatically. It simply awakens the cells in your body to what they already know. They know The Truth, and when you consciously know it too, every part of your being is given permission to work as one in order to be powerful again. For this reason it is a form of *cellular knowing*. This means there is no need to follow routines, steps or lists of things to do. The Truth transforms you without even trying. It re-forms and re-covers you. Deep down, you subconsciously enable your entire being to harmonize and flow. All you need to do is know The Truth, and then just trust whatever unfolds from your new way of seeing and being.

It needs to be noted that we are forming a new language through our journey together. We do this in order to simplify The Truth, give it clarity, and most importantly avoid the dogma, doctrine, influence, opinion and sentiment associated with established language.

Throughout history, many of mankind's most powerful teachings or messages have become lost in language, translation and interpretation. We can also overcomplicate vital messages through language, distorting them so they lose their power and vitality.

Our new language will unite us and empower us, both individually and collectively.

Language shapes the way we think, and determines what we can think about.
Benjamin Lee Whorf

This section will guide you through crucial stages of the most powerful discovery you can make. You will rediscover and recover your True Self further, using reminders that keep you on track. You will also begin to see the obstacles that can get in your way, or block your strength, joy and vitality. Then, when you are ready, you will set your Self free, to confidently take flight from the refuge in this growing place. You will face the world with wings you never knew you had.

2.1

Forming New Foundations

You are now re-forming your Self, and you are replacing Destructive Imposed and Foundational Connections with new Life-Generating ones. This powerful knowing will not conflict with any Life-Generating religion, culture or creed. In fact, this message aligns exquisitely with every pure religion. And it supports the lessons and secrets to be learned from indigenous cultures that have survived in harmony with each other and the planet over centuries.

Be careful though. There will be a temptation to apply this powerful new knowing to your existing vocabulary. The problem with this is words and phrases hold all kinds of sentiment. And those feelings can be both destructive and constructive, depending on individual Foundational Connections. So it's best that we avoid using existing language. To transform, we need new words and phrases that hold clean energy.

Language holds energy. It serves to re-mind you, keeping you connected to what matters most. And it has the power to unite us all.

See if you are able to resist the temptation to re-language this message. Share it with those in your existing communities. And see if you are able to use this message and the untainted language it uses, to unite you, especially with those who belong to different cultures, religions, creeds or societies.

Below we look at some of the basic principles of this message, and we continue to create the language that will unite, protect and free us.

We must be prepared to consider radically new views of reality.
Basil Hiley

2.1.1   Illusionary Self

Let's start by creating a common term for the false sense of your Self you are given by those around you and society. As you now know, that 'you' is in fact the opposite of *who you really are*: it's an entranced, autopilot version of your True Self. This 'self' is a learned, habitual way of thinking and being that has nothing to do with your True Self. It simply reflects historical patterns imposed upon you. And it can be released the minute you see it for what it is.

Because this view on your Self is actually an illusion, we will call it your *Illusionary Self*.

When you think you are your shell, appearance, your mind, thoughts, circumstances or past, socioeconomic status, social standing, culture, religion, or job, then you have lost your powerful *Core Self* to a trick of the mind. This belief will de-form, mis-direct and dis-connect you from all that matters and everything that fulfills you.

But ending the cycle is so simple. All you need to do is know *differently.*

Know The Truth and it will set you free.

A human being is part of the whole called by us the universe,
a part limited in time and space.
He experiences himself, his thoughts and feelings, as something separated from the rest,
a kind of optical delusion of his consciousness.
Albert Einstein

2.1.2   Core Creator Self

As you have now discovered, at a Core level, you are *Life-Generating Energy.* You are connected to, and part of, the greatest living force in the universe. So when discussing this True Powerful You, we need to use a term that represents The Truth. Because you are self-creating and *Life-Generating* at your Core, let's call your

True Self your *Core Creator Self* or *Core Self*. However, we will discover all kinds of other powerful terms for your Core Self as we travel together, in order for you to find one, or a few, that work for you.

It's also important to be careful not to get stuck in labels. Remember, labels can define and confine you. And don't forget, your Source Self does not speak in words, but rather in sentiment, or feeling. Therefore, if at any time, there is an association with a word or phase that holds negative sentiment for you, please simply change it to work with what *feels* right for you. The same word can mean many different things to different people. What matters most is to ensure your words correspond with your inner Truth, support positive feelings, and empower you.

Words hold sentiment and great power – we need to respect the power they hold and use them carefully and cautiously. They affect both those who speak them and those who hear them.

Throughout our discovery together, we will therefore use terms such as Essence Self, True You, Real You, Source Self, Powerful Essence, the 'you' you were born to be, and any other words or phrases that reflect *who you really are*.

Remember, the greatest connection you can make is to your Authentic Self, as through this connection you will be connected to all life and to the ultimate Source of all life. And in order to be connected to this *Core Creator Self*, you simply need to feel connected. Trust your feelings.

2.1.3   Connecting to Life-Generating Energy

Central to The Truth message is *The Power of Connection*. As we have discovered, life is simply a series of connections. And every connection we make comes under one of two headings:

> *Life-Generating Connections*, or
> *Life-Depleting Connections*.

All connections hold energy. So all connections carry either:

> *Life-Generating Energy*, or
> *Life-Depleting Energy*.

As we are elementally Life-Generating Energy at our essence, if we make Life-Generating Connections we will grow and flourish. And if we make Life-Depleting Connections we will wither, shrink and diminish our Selves.

Anything that grows you and others is Life-Generating. Anything that hurts, destroys, disrespects, depreciates or harms your Self or others, emotionally or physically, is Life-Depleting.

Even though Life-Depleting action is destructive to all, it is more destructive to those creating, expressing and enabling it than it is to those it targets.

In order to thrive, connect to and engage in what is Life-Generating and avoid or prevent what is Life-Depleting in any way you can.

It really is that simple.

2.1.4   Source Energy Connection

Source Energy is your ultimate propeller, motor, radar, navigator and engine. It's the wind beneath your sails. It provides the air pocket that will take you beyond your wildest dreams. It is what keeps you buoyant and winged. It strengthens you and completes you. Without a connection to Source Energy, you must remain grounded, for only through a connection to Source Energy can you make a connection to the atmosphere that keeps you airborne. You can therefore never "fly" into the realm of *I'm-possibility* without a deep, profound and genuine connection to Source Energy.

Some people connect to Source Energy through religion. Others disconnect from Source Energy through religion. Fear tactics used by some religions to drive an agenda or exert control is the antithesis of Source Energy, or what religions often refer to as God. Source Energy is Love-driven. And power, fear or division is the opposite of Love.

All religions, *in their pure form*, will tell you God is Love. And power, fear, division, judgment, oppression, hatred and self-righteousness are the opposite of Love. So going to war, for example, in the name of religion, is a complete contradiction. No pure religious leader would ever support this.

We need to look at the groups we are part of, including the religious groups, and examine what they are doing. If they have a Love-directed, Life-Generating focus that accepts and respects others, they are legitimate. If they are driven by self-righteous directives that are judgmental, or are 'sin' or punishment focused, then we can be confident that The Truth and pure message of their original faith has been lost.

How we connect to Source Energy is irrelevant. What matters is that we connect. That is all that matters.

True religion has a universal quality.
It does not find fault with other religions.
Forgiveness, compassion, tolerance, brotherhood
and the feeling of oneness
are the signs of a true religion.
Sri Chinmoy

2.1.5   Eternally Free

Once we know how to metaphorically fly, allowing our Selves to connect to and be carried by the ultimate driving force of all life, Source Energy, we will always fly – even when we die.

You are not your body or your exterior. The Truth is you are none of the things you can see, touch, taste or sense physically. Those things are simply part of your current experience. You are unlimited Energy experiencing life within the constraints of a human body for a period of time we call a lifetime. But it's not your lifetime. You existed, energetically, before you were conceived. You were part of the ultimate Source Energy – being no-thing and every-thing all at once. What this means is when your body breaks down, your

Energy will be as free as it was before your conception – it will be unlimited and infinite.

So what we call dying is simply our Energy departing our body. Our body is discarded, like a shell, and we leave this physical realm. But we are Energy! So we never actually end – we never die. When we become guided and guarded by our Source, we sense this knowing deep down. We feel eternally free, even in our embodied form, which we know will eventually evolve or change. That is why there is really nothing to fear.

We need not fear death, for it is simply the next phase of life. We never die, we simply change form – just as we have since the day we were born.

The Truth is Source Energy flies you – no matter what your form – after you 'die' and before you were born.

Seeing death as the end of life is like seeing the horizon as the end of the ocean.
David Searls

Those who have had 'near-death experiences' provide evidence of this knowing: they suddenly experience The Truth, and it transforms them forever.

For example, Anita Moorjani, in her book, Dying to be Me (2012) reveals how, after four years of fighting cancer, her organs began to shut down and she entered into an extraordinary near-death experience, which changed her life. She describes how she was able to 'see' everything about her life, past and present, including what her loved ones were thinking or feeling, all at the same time. Everything she experienced happened at once, simultaneously. Nothing was linear. She described her 'seeing' as an "energy sense rather than a seeing sense". She felt her Self as pure consciousness – huge, powerful, expanded – in this energetic state. She looked at her body and it just felt so "small, lifeless, limp, insignificant". There was a sense of wonderment: how can this insignificant thing house this: what I'm feeling now? There was no sequential order to anything. Everything was parallel in time, somewhat like a dream. She found that the further she stepped back, the more she could see the order of the grander scheme. She realized that the essence of who she is never truly dies, regardless of what it looks like.

After thirty hours in this place, or space, which felt timeless to Moorjani, she got to the point where she felt she was given the choice to come back, or not. There was no judgment. All she felt, from those who had passed over, and from every-one and every-thing, was unconditional love.

She decided to return to her body and was released from hospital weeks later – without a trace of the cancer that had riddled her organs.

It wasn't my beliefs that caused me to heal.
My NDE (near-death experience) was a state of pure awareness,
which is a state of complete suspension of all previously held doctrine and dogma.
This allowed my body to 'reset' itself.
In other words, an absence of belief was required for my healing.
Anita Moorjani

Another way to word this is that Anita Moorjani healed her body, or her current 'vehicle', by entering into the pure essence of who she really is. She entered the *Empty Space* – the every-thing and no-thing that she was before she began being in her body; and the every-thing and no-thing that she always will be, regardless of whether she is embodied or not.

2.1.6   Being One

When we understand that we are intrinsically connected to and part of the greatest Energy generating all life, we expand our Selves. We expand our Selves beyond our current form. We expand our Selves into the Energy we were before we were our current form – and also into the Energy we will be once we leave this form. We become comfortable and familiar with *who we really are*, despite the limitations of our body, or vehicle. This is the most liberating way to live.

Through this understanding, we begin to see that both you and I came from the same omnipresent Cardinal Energy Source. So we are in fact simply expressed forms of the same Energy. WE are separate embodied forms of the One Greater Energy. And WE will both return to this shared Energy Source once our current realm of reality emerges into the next.

When we see this we also see that destruction of any life is in fact at the deepest level, our own destruction. And what we create, we live with, live in and go back to. This understanding is where the concept of karma originated – and even the concept of "hell". However, like much of religion, these concepts which were developed to keep us doing good, have repeatedly been distorted and misrepresented by some religious groups to suit individual Foundational Connections and agendas.

What matters is only this: To destroy, diminish or devalue others is to destroy, diminish and devalue your deepest Self or Essence.

To live a life that is Life-Generating connects you to the Core of *who you really are*, and to the Source of all Living Energy. This ensures that your Core Creator Self is constantly connected to the Energy of

All Existence and to unlimited possibility. It keeps your Inner Energy Centre vital and powerful – whether you are in an embodied form or not. Then the natural process of death becomes something to be revered rather than feared. It becomes the ultimate *passage through*, back to your Elemental Source – back to the ultimate Source of all life, back to the everything and no-thing that unites every one of us.

2.2

Clearing the Way to a New You

To break free from the limitations of your *Imposed* and *Foundational Connections* and release your powerful essence, we need to address a few potential obstacles that may become a barrier to living the life you long for.

2.2.1   Brain Babble

A big barrier to living your freedom lies in something we can call *Brain Babble.*

Brain Babble is that little voice in your mind, which constantly analyses, questions, judges, compares, values, assesses, fears, fantasizes, comforts, regrets, worries and so the list goes on. We all have it.

Many of us believe this voice is who we are; we think it is our self, talking to us. And that is the worst thing we can do.
It is not you. It is simply your brain doing what brains and minds do. Just as your kidneys or liver work constantly to filter toxins and

eliminate waste, so does the organ we call your brain. The only difference between the automatic function of the kidney, and the brain, is you can 'hear' your brain functioning. And through this 'hearing' process, you are given the ultimate steering wheel – you can choose to engage certain ideas, thoughts or directives, and you can choose to ignore others.

You see, this voice is actually a regurgitation of your connections to date. It is your mind offering you a direction, so you can either allow a particular navigation route, or not. It reflects life around you and picks up input just as an out-of-tune radio station might. It actually has nothing to do with *who you really are*, but rather what you have been exposed to, experienced, or seen, in this embodied form. Therefore, what you have 'decided to believe' is simply a choice you have made – a choice you can change at any time.

Unless you tune in to a thought, sentiment, belief or directive, babble will be powerless.

So, until you direct this voice it is simply meaningless babble. That is why we call it *Brain Babble*.

Brain Babble can however provide a fascinating insight into repeated patterns of allowed or connected 'thinking'.

If you focus on or engage in a particular 'thought' your mind sees that as a "yes, keep this directive". So that thought will repeat itself. Then it will begin to grow, and it will direct and grow you.

What you focus on grows.

What you connect to will take over you.

For this reason, if you simply make a note of your *Brain Babble* for a day, or perhaps even a few days, you will likely see patterns emerging. When you do this, it is important to just observe – without judgment. Jot down your babble, or 'thoughts'. Then afterwards, look over your notes, and you will begin to see what's been directing your life. You will see what you are holding on to. And you will receive some great insights about why you are where you are right now.

This is liberating, as if you don't like what you see, you can change it, instantly.

See if you can simply allow *Brain Babble* to come, and to go. Only focus on, or hold on, to that which grows you and others in positive constructive ways. See the rest like you would a billboard on the side of the road: a distraction that you walk right past without a second thought. Only engage with what feeds your True Self – your Love-directed Centre – as that will feed all life, especially yours.

Trying to block out or fight Brain Babble engages it and empowers it, just as entering a boxing arena makes a connection with a fighter.

We simply need to give unwanted *Brain Babble* no attention, realizing it's just a function of the organ called your brain or mind. It is not you. It has nothing to do with your Essence. This is the passage to inner peace and the goal of practices like meditation and yoga. When you disconnect from *Brain Babble*, you reconnect to your True Self – and to all Living Energy, at a root level.

Brain Babble can only affect you if you listen to it, act upon it, believe it, hold on to it, or try to make it go away.

Yoga and meditation are unlikely to be effective without this understanding because people who regard their babble as their innermost thinking or even an expression of themselves, will feel they are shutting themselves out by ignoring this voice. It is difficult to silence something we believe is intrinsic to who we are. The Truth is anyone can meditate, anywhere, in any position, without a teacher, without a class, if they simply sit silently with their True

Inner Self, allowing themselves to feel and connect to the Greater Energy within them, and around them, and allowing the *Brain Babble* to come, and go, without any emotional response or connection. Anyone can connect, any time, anywhere, to their inner peace, powerful Essence and Greater Life Source even in the midst of a crowded room.

Peace.
It does not mean to be in a place where there is no noise, trouble or hard work.
It means to be in the midst of these things and still be calm in your heart.
Source Unknown

Jill Bolte Taylor is a brain scientist who was struck suddenly by a stroke. She recounted her experience in A Stroke of Insight (2009). Taylor's journey provides a rare insight into how the mind, consciousness and our energy interconnect, intersect and distort one another. Taylor recounts how when the left side of her brain shut down, what she had always known as her inner chatter – what we would call Brain Babble – stopped. There was no-thing, Empty Space, silence. Taylor explains the lightness, peace, nirvana and serenity here, in this silent place. She, as a brain scientist, saw it as her right brain – her intuitive, non-logical consciousness. But perhaps, like Moorjani, what she was experiencing was the incredible liberation of her pure True Self – her Core Energetic Self, uncluttered by the non-sense, the Babble and the distractions.

Like Moorjani, Taylor describes the same sense of one-ness, beauty and interconnectedness of everything and everyone. She felt in awe of the tranquility, the pure bliss and the enlightenment she experienced so fully. In the eight years it took her to completely recover from her stroke, her view of her Self and life around became powerfully transformed.

Our 'mind' represents our programming. Our 'brain' is matter – part of the matter that contains this programming. But we are beyond both.

Mind is consciousness which has put on limitations.
You are originally unlimited and perfect.
Later you take on limitation and become the mind.
Ramana Maharshi

2.2.2   SOUL Food

We all know the old saying, "you are what you eat". And of course it is true, we don't put unhealthy food into our bodies and expect them to be healthy. What we may not realize is that regardless of how well we eat, we will never feel complete, Whole or healthy at an elemental level, unless we are feeding our Energy Essence with healthy Energy 'food', which we can call Soul Food.

If we allow our Energy to be directed by and connected to Soul-less or destructive pursuits, we will feel diminished and depleted no matter how well we eat.

It is vitally important to your vitality and wellbeing that, as much as is possible, you only engage in and connect to that which feeds your SOUL, or your Essence – in other words that which is Life-Generating and Love-directed.

Every movie, music clip, song, news show, documentary, cartoon, magazine, conversation, internet site, social media app, video, computer game or book can either feed you or deplete you. If what you engage in involves gossip, violence, aggression, explicit or disconnected sex, exploitation, disrespectful language or a glorification of the Illusionary Self such as image, money, brands, looks or other forms of superficial social engineering, then it will be disconnecting and diminishing you.

The Truth is that it is even more important for us to feed our Soul healthy Soul Food than it is to feed our body healthy edible food. The reason being our bodies can more easily eliminate toxins and waste. What we put into our Soul, however, what we engage in or connect to Energetically, changes our Energy. And we are elementally Energy. So the food we eat effects our body, or the vehicle we use to get around in. But what we take in at an energetic level changes who we are being: what we do, where we go and what we become.

If you take in violence, it will violate you.

If you play with destruction, it will destroy you.

If you believe lies, The Truth cannot set you free.

When you know The Truth, you will see with great clarity that society surrounds us and even bombards us with toxic Soul Food. And then, armed with clear vision, you will naturally and automatically avoid the traps.

Most importantly, children need adults to protect and shield them from toxic Soul Food. We need to boycott violent or disturbing children's movies, books, magazines and games. We need to Love and nurture our children, ignoring anyone who tells us otherwise. Using verbal, physical or psychological aggression to raise children is destructive to the extreme. Likewise, emotional or physical neglect, exploitation or manipulation of children is something we must do all we can to stop. We need to reconnect our young to their inner Essence and power, protecting them from all that disconnects and diminishes them. This is the greatest thing we can do for our children, and for humanity.

It has never been more important to be vigilant about what we take in to our Energy than it is now. Technology has the capacity to destroy or revolutionize us, as individuals, as a human race, and as a planet. Through a vast technological web of connection that knows no boundaries, we have been given the ultimate tool, the most incredible opportunity, or the beginning of our demise. We can use this opportunity to unite and grow us like never before. It's entirely up to us. What we can be certain of is how we use this tool will determine our future and fate.

And every little thing you or I do matters. WE all feed and fuel the directive. Our world now offers a plethora of connections, suddenly available at the tip of our fingers. What we choose to watch, share, read or engage in has the capacity to transform the human race beyond our imagination, at lightning speed. If we connect to what is Life-Depleting we will self-destruct before we know it. If we only choose that which is Life-Generating we will transcend our wildest dreams and create an unimaginable future of possibility for our children, never seen on earth before.

Watch what you eat by all means. But much more importantly, watch what you feed your Soul.

The core of every fruit is better than its rind.
Regard the body as the rind, and the human spirit the core.
Rumi

2.2.3   Nature Naturally Restores

Every living being on the planet came into being from the same Source.   All life began in a spontaneous moment, through the connection or union of two individual entities.   And there was an underlying Energy, called Source Energy, which generated that connection, the next connection and the following series of connections until finally a living being came into being independently.

Therefore, every one of us is essentially as individual as each cell in our body.   We are all an individual part of One greater Life Force, from which each of our lives was generated, and of which we are all a part.   So, you can imagine your Self as an individual cell in the greater body of life.   And the greater body of life is the planet surrounding you – or even the entire universe.   To forget this is to disconnect from your Core, which is the inner manifestation of all of this, and of all that is – it connects you to your greatest strength, power and limitlessness.   So to connect to your Core Self is to connect to all life, and to connect to all life is to connect to your Core.   Your Essence is the same Essence of all life.   Connect deeply

90

to either, your Core or life around you, and you fuse you with the Core Source Energy of the universe – the ultimate driving force of nature and of every living thing, of which you are a part.

This is why when we connect to nature and focus intently on the flow and rhythm of the ocean, a spider as it weaves its intricate and genius web, the softness and scent of fresh green grass as it protects and comforts the soles of our bare feet, a rainbow as it brightens a moody sky, or a butterfly as it flutters its delicate wings magically navigating through space, we stimulate and reinvigorate our Selves at a cardinal level. We enliven our Selves.

Connecting to the rhythm of nature reconnects you to your own life rhythm.

While we act in harmony with life around us, we replenish, inspire and exhilarate our True Self. And if we are destructive to life around us, it would be as destructive as a cell in our own body attacking surrounding cells – we call that cancer.

So to connect to nature, to sit with it and in it, to appreciate it, to hear it, smell it, sense it, and to value it, strengthens and grows us at our deepest Core level. To act in harmony with nature keeps us well. It recovers us. It connects us to our real Self. This is why nature naturally restores.

With our culture becoming more mechanized, and society being increasingly dominated by technology, we risk losing what we need most.

See if you are able to escape the buildings, the concrete, and the man-made trappings, regularly. Take your Self into the sanctuary of your Soul through reconnecting as much as possible with nature – even if it's only for a few minutes each day. Switch off the television, turn off the computers, and take your Self to a park, the beach or a garden. Sit on the sand and let nature reconnect and revitalize you. Nature feeds and fuels you. It's vital to your vitality. And if you have children, they depend on you to feed and fuel them with the gifts of nature as much as possible.

You will feel different when you regularly consciously appreciate and focus on the natural world around you – the calmness and gentle motion of the trees, the grace, genius and mystery of the bird in flight, the beauty and fragrance of flowers, the vast magnificence of the sky or the warmth and comfort of the sun.

You will begin to feel more energized by an intrinsic inner knowing and powerful life force. The more you connect to and nurture nature, the more connected and nurtured you will feel at a deep level. Then you will find your Self naturally resisting that which depletes you. You will automatically begin to choose powerfully Life-Generating Soul Food and Brain Babble. And you will look

back in awe at the effortlessness with which you evolved. What a
magnificently simple revelation.

I love to think of nature as an unlimited broadcasting station,
through which God speaks to us every hour,
if we will only tune in.
George Washington Carver

2.3

Simple Reminders

Below are a few simple reminders that you can use to reinvigorate your Powerful Essence. If you feel lost, disorientated or disconnected, use the following tools to recover your Core Self and direct you back to *who you really are* and what you most need.

2.3.1   S O U L

You don't have a soul. You are a Soul. You have a body.
C.S. Lewis

Let us start with a simple acronym that serves to keep you connected to, and directed by, your powerful Essence. It acts as a quick checklist which you can use any time to examine your actions and ensure they align with the magic of *I'm-possibility*. The point is to check that you are engaging all four elements of this acronym in all you do.

Aptly named *SOUL*, there are four components, which we will discuss independently. They are:

Spontaneous

Open

Uninhibited

Love

Keep a SOUL focus and life with amaze you.

When you do things from your soul you feel a river moving in you.
Rumi

Spontaneous

Many of us, in our modern world, have lost the art of Spontaneity. And Spontaneity is required to keep us connected to the flow of life around us. Through it, we become a droplet in the tide of life, carried to the most incredible shores.

To be Spontaneous is to trust the process and unfolding of life. You allow life to carry you, accepting and respecting where it takes you. See if you can listen to your instincts and trust your deepest knowing, going and flowing with and through the ever evolving shifting, without judgment. Do and be Life-Generating, no matter what happens. Express your Self fully and say what you feel, honestly and with Love. Allow your Self to be caught in a moment, and moved or touched by events, situations and people. See if you can allow your Self to get caught up in life, in the milliseconds of life, take it all in, every minute detail, just as a curious child discovers an insect with reverence.

Spontaneity requires you to let go of your insecurities and constant questioning. Your Brain Babble takes a back seat. You are able to choose what feels right in the moment, trusting your feelings over logical 'thinking'. So it's an extremely liberating way of being. It frees you to just be. It's about being un-reasonable, trusting the process of life and your deep inner calling or knowing over what seems reasonable.

Life will surprise you, exceeding your wildest dreams and surpassing your most ambitious plans – if you are able to stay connected to your Core Self, Source Energy and all that is Life-Generating. So hold on to this as your greatest strength.

Have goals by all means, but try not to hold onto them rigidly. Allow your plans to evolve and flow, with life around you, and don't be surprised when you look back in hindsight at how your original plans morphed into unimaginably brilliant manifestations.

Remind your Self that control is an illusion, and the more of it we think we have the less we really do have. Ironically, you will feel more in control than ever when you hand over the reigns to Source Energy – and *trust* life itself.

Try to let life be. Allow people, situations, circumstances and phases of your life to come, and to go. Flow with life, and if something doesn't feel right, move on, Lovingly, graciously and gratefully.

Life is a series of natural and spontaneous changes.
Don't resist them; that only creates sorrow.
Let reality be reality.
Let things flow naturally forward in whatever way they like.
Lao Tzu

Don't think too much. Just trust. And see where life takes you.
You will be amazed.

Open

When we are Open, we Open our hearts to those around us. We refuse to shut our True Essence down, even and especially when we feel betrayed, hurt, used, abandoned or rejected. When we are Open, we know others are simply projecting their unconscious *Foundational Connections*. We hold empathy and compassion for those who are lost, rather than judgment. And we resist the temptation to join destructive cycles, or to become resigned, cynical or bitter.

Being Open is about not allowing the energy of those around you to change your Energy. It's about holding on to your Love Center and Life-Generating focus.

An Open heart allows us to be self-expressed, to feel our feelings, and show them to others. We are able to share our passions and our True Self. We are able to be authentic, real and deeply connected to others, through honesty, integrity and sharing. We let those we love know how we feel about them.

To be Open, we also become Open to whatever transpires. We resist deciding what 'should' occur. We trust that if we come from a Love-directed place, life will unfold perfectly – even when relationships end, or when we are hurt, shocked or upset by what occurs. We are always growing and learning, at every level, and sometimes it can be a difficult or painful process. When we are Open we welcome all growth and evolution, even the painful bits. We walk away from what is Life-Depleting. We refuse to engage in destruction, and we protect our Pure Essence, regardless of what comes our way. Then, our Love focus will attract exactly what we need to recover.

Being Open opens doors.

Uninhibited

Being Uninhibited is about being liberated, free-spirited and unencumbered by the facades of life. It requires us to resist the temptation to hide our Selves in our consumerist world, behind brands, false social media sites and other superficial veneers. Being Uninhibited is not about recklessness or out of control behavior. In fact it's about authenticity. It's about expressing our deepest Self, in a Loving, kind and genuine way.

To be Uninhibited frees us to be truly honest, and to speak and be our truth. Our words, actions and thoughts align. We are congruent, and live with integrity. We rid our Selves of concerns about what others may think. We express our Selves fully. Although we may feel a little vulnerable at first, being Uninhibited actually secures us in our relationships because the only way to truly have a deep connection with another is to show them *who you really are.*

Being Uninhibited is about congruence and free self-expression – it's about our actions and words aligning.

When we are Uninhibited, we no longer repress The Truth. We no longer pretend. We express our inner truth, even when it means admitting we feel differently, or that we have made a mistake. We speak up about what matters, facing the consequences without fear. Unconcerned about the judgment of others, or even ridicule, we do what matters, we say what matters, and we be what matters. We are able to be a voice for the voiceless. We take the stand, we make a stand, and we do it for the good of all. We take responsibility, and we do all we can to Lovingly restore any damage we may have caused. There is nothing to prove when you live in this way. You are free to be exactly *who you really are.*

The brilliant thing about being Uninhibited is you no longer need to pretend, or hide away from the "painful" or confronting aspects of your ever-unfolding evolution. You can confidently embrace, share and grow through your challenges.

Authentic expression, from a place of Love, marks the noblest of individuals.

Happiness is when what you think, what you say, and what you do are in harmony.
Gandhi

Love

All four elements of this acronym overflow and interact, just as life itself does. But the thread that ties it all together is Love. No matter what you do, say or be, ensure you are coming from your Love-directed Core. This is the critical element of SOUL, and it will ensure you remain connected to your True Essence, and Whole.

Many of us see Love, mistakenly, as a passive way of being. We may believe that to act from Love is to accept dysfunction, or even destruction, aggression or violence. This is not Love. Love is about having the strength to resist becoming part of anything destructive, reflecting it away from you, making a stand for what is Love-directed, and keeping your SOUL pure. It requires you to retain a Love-directed focus. And it also requires you to have the strength to be Uninhibited – to Spontaneously respond to dysfunction and destruction, with confidence and with passion. So, for example, if someone attacked you physically, you would not stand there passively, nor would you strike back – instead you would stand your ground, redirecting or reflecting their aggression away from you like a martial arts move. You would not take the destructive force on; you would not take it in, even if you were struck.

No one can hurt me without my permission.
Gandhi

By moving aggression, or dysfunction, away from you, you are stepping out of a destructive process. You are no longer feeding, or enabling, a destructive cycle. To allow dysfunction to continue, you are allowing those creating the dysfunction to deplete themselves, and you. To turn away, redirect, reflect, or disallow destruction is to grow others, including those behaving in destructive ways. To grow others grows you. To deplete others depletes you.

Love in action depletes, disengages disconnects and disables destruction.

Love is your vitality. To do things that are Life-Generating is to act from a place of Love. And this is what enables you. This is how you grow. This is how you find your passion, your deepest purpose, your sense of meaning and belonging. Acting, thinking, doing and being with Love feeds you, grows you and fulfills you. Love expands, transforms and enables you in unimaginable ways. It awakens your calling. And Love in action feeds every life around you – that's the truly magnificent part of this process. Being Loving, kind and compassionate, supporting and growing life around you, not only feeds and grows you, it also creates a new world.

At an elemental level you are Pure Love, so Love is your ultimate feeder.

One word frees us from all the weight and pain of life: that word is love.
Sophocles

2.3.2 The 3 G'S to Happiness

The Truth is, in order to be truly happy and fulfilled we need to be:

Generous

Gracious

Grateful

When you feel unhappy, empty or out of integrity, despite the fact that you are attempting to be SOUL directed, you can be sure one of these elements will be missing. The Truth is without the 3 G's you cannot be entirely Love-directed. All you need to do is simply ask your Self which one of the 3 G's is missing from your focus, sentiment or way of being. Then change your focus, and this will change your being, so joy can flow back to you effortlessly.

Generosity

For those of us who are fortunate enough to live in a privileged society, it is our duty to give back and to share our good fortune. We owe it to the greater body of our Existence. When we exist purely for ourselves, or for our direct family for example, we become bloated and distended. We actually become a heavy weight to our Selves. And we begin to sink in the tide of life that is designed to carry us and keep us buoyant.

At a deep level, exclusive personal self-indulgence, whether it be materially, emotionally, physically, is one of the most disconnecting things we can do to our Selves. Our True Self knows that elementally we are connected to every body else, so if we luxuriate exclusively, or consume obliviously, we disassociate from every body else – we disconnect from the greater body of which we are a part.

Therefore, every self-centered self-indulgence further separates us from what we need to be happy. It dis-associates us from others, from our Powerful Core Essence, and from the sense of connection we need to feel and be fulfilled. We lose our sense of Self to a sense of self-entitlement. We, through our actions, are rendering ourselves more valuable than, and separate to, those around us. And then, at a deeply unconscious and fundamental level, we are no longer able to be part of all life around us – which is where our power, fulfillment and true sense of meaning lies. This is why those who become rich and famous often also become extremely unhappy.

It is important to know that ownership is an illusion. One day, we will all change form, and our bodies will cease to be. Then all those 'things' we've indulged in, accumulated, or defined ourselves though, will become someone else's, or they will perish like our bodies. Why not make whatever you can someone else's now, while you can share in the joy that spreads. Then the joy you share will feed and enable you. It will grow the world you live in. The material gains we feel define us are simply confining us to our Illusionary Self. What we truly need is to be connected to our Core Self and to the Energy of all life. And giving, sharing, generosity and thoughtfulness keeps us connected.

Some people say, "I'm not a good gift-giver", or, "I don't cope well with looking after sick people". These are examples of the excuses some of us use to exclusively self indulge. This Brain Babble is not only untrue, but it destroys those who believe it. We can all give thoughtfully and generously. It's a choice we make. And that choice has a bigger impact on our happiness than it does on anyone else's.

The 'all-for-me-and-only-me' mentality is the most destructive force on earth.

Unfortunately, many people who come into money suddenly believe their wealth gives them some kind of status, value or importance. The Truth is money does give us power, but if we misuse this power we are allowing it to overpower and destroy us. This is why, ironically, often people who have fallen into affluence give abundantly to other wealthy or "high status" people, while remaining tightfisted or stingy with others. They do this because they believe giving to influential people will buy them favor or respect. The problem is this then becomes just another self-indulgent purchase. In a material world we can get caught up in this trap unknowingly. Companies often engage in this kind of activity, giving to celebrities and influential clients while making no contribution to the needy. It's simply a commercial decision. We need to be careful. We can convince ourselves we are being generous, when in fact we are connecting to, feeding and growing what is completely SOUL-less.

Sonja was frustrated and extremely depressed before she discovered The Truth. She attended numerous yoga retreats, visited her natural therapist, counselor and healer every week, invested in "soul workshops", read countless self-help books and attended seminars and meditation sessions – all in vain. She felt increasingly lost, despite the wealth that her husband was building around her. She attended charity functions where she would bump into prominent people, and often she would give generously at these functions – to impress. She spent money effortlessly on herself, her home, her children and her "high ranking" financially well off friends, but that's where her generosity ended. Increasingly, she felt empty and depleted. Then, she discovered the 3 G's. She broke down in tears as she looked at her life.

"I'd drive in my luxury car, wear expensive designer clothes, and spoil my rich friends with extravagant gifts, but I told myself I was 'too poor' to support my elderly father financially in any major way. What was I thinking?" Sonja was dismayed that she had failed to see something so obvious. "What is money for if it's not to spoil those I love and care about, and to do good? How could I have become

106

so SOUL-less? Even what I called my spiritual life was simply a self indulgence."

Sonja thankfully had woken up. She realized that all those high profile friends were actually not friends at all. They were connected to the same SOUL-less pursuits and were never going to provide the fulfilling relationships she needed. She fixed her father's appalling living conditions. She called the friends and family members she had neglected, explaining her breakthrough and apologizing for her behavior. She began helping people in need, anonymously, she began to campaign for animal rights, and she gave generously to those she truly valued and cared about. She had never been happier in her life. And her Energy transformed instantly. She began to really shine, and it was tangible to everyone.

For those who recognize their own patterns here, congratulations! It's time to break free. This cycle is SOUL-less and destructive. It takes courage to see The Truth but it will set you free if you let it.

Generosity is about generosity of spirit. So it's also about forgiving others and accepting that we are all learners, and therefore we all make mistakes. Without connecting to those who are on a destructive path, we find happiness flows our way when we are able to find it in our hearts to help and support those around us rather than condemn them – even and especially those who challenge us.

Giving connects us to our joy as much as unshared personal indulgence disconnects us from it.

---

*The miracle that happens every time to those who really love:
the more they give, the more they possess.*
Rainer Marie Rilke

Grace

Pride disrupts the ride of your life.

Grace is about being humble. It's about empathetically considering the needs of others, even when those needs compromise your pride, ego or sense of self-righteousness.

When you live your life SOUL-fully, and you know that you are part of every living being at the most fundamental level, you realize you are no better and no worse than anyone else. You do not have different standards for yourself. You realize that what you value, other people do too. And you have the same amount of respect for another's life as you do for your own. You know you are not more

108

entitled than anybody else. You treat all life with the same respect and dignity you would your Self.

Living graciously is about humility. There is no judgment. We do not exploit, use, abuse or scorn others. We Love, accept and understand. And that doesn't mean we stand by and watch destruction. In fact, when we operate from a place of Love and Grace, we do all we can to stop Life-Depleting action and destruction. But we do it Lovingly, peacefully and with strength and determined humility.

Grace is fantastically liberating as we can let self-righteousness, ego and pride go, knowing they are simply Illusionary Self reflections. They distract us from our happiness. They have nothing to do with *who you really are.*

Grace allows us to freely admit fault, saying sorry genuinely when we make mistakes, and taking responsibility for our actions. It requires a WE-llness as opposed to an I-llness focus: an other-focus rather than a self-focus. Living with Grace therefore allows you to see the other person's point of view, and accept genuinely, even when it opposes your views.

With Grace, you are also able to graciously accept the flow of life – even when what you want to happen doesn't. Grace gives you the freedom to realize resolutions and solutions are not always the resolutions and solutions you may want or expect. To be gracious enough to accept life, and respect others, SOUL-fully, allows joy to flow over you like a waterfall. It washes you clean.

Grace allows us to see that as part of every body else, we are not more worthy or important, and that we grow through sharing, caring and growing others.

This is why when we put our Selves on a pedestal above others we instantly become lost in an inward, Illusionary Self focus. We can unknowing sabotage our happiness in this simple way. We seek celebrity status, or fame, only to find it destroys us. If we are able to resist the temptation to be adored, or adorned, we will retain Grace, humility and dignity – and in doing so we will maintain deep inner fulfillment and happiness.

This isn't to say that we can't be leaders, social change advocates and great examples. In fact, to live SOUL-fully we need to be all three. But we can do so with humility. We can refuse to take on any grand social status that may come our way. We can see our work as an act of Love that is greater than any one individual. Look at those who really did make a difference, and displayed enormous power to create incredible change – Gandhi and Mother Teresa for example. They shunned and dismissed adulation.

The best way to find yourself is to lose yourself in the service of others.
Gandhi

We are pencils in the hand of God.
Mother Teresa

A true "guru" will not take on a guru status.

Grace takes us out of the small picture of our Selves. It takes us into the realm of greater knowing and magnificent connection. It brings synchronicity to us, and Opens doors. It's a universal language of Love and acceptance. Grace sets us free and washes us clean.

See if you can rest upon the wings of Grace. Let it lighten your load as it lifts you to the greatest heights, taking you where you most need to go.

THE TRUTH AD INFINITUM

Gratitude

---

*He is a wise man who does not grieve for the things which he has not,
but rejoices for those which he has.*
Epicetus

Regardless of our circumstances, we can always find reason to be Grateful – even if it is simply for the air we breathe, the experience of life itself, or the reading of these words and the ability to be part of a global revolution.

It can be confronting to experience the joy in the faces of children living in poor conditions compared to rich Western children. Happiness oozes from the little human beings who live a simple life, while those who have so much materially often appear comparatively apathetic and joyless. And the reason why is simple. The 'underprivileged' children are part of a community where they share food, shelter, nurture and care. They have a sense of belonging that is lost in the West through an Illusionary Self focus. They are inter-dependent, just as they need to be, rather than independent. They practice Generosity, Grace and Gratitude as part of their daily life. They give to one another, they consider themselves equal and they are Grateful for the help they receive from one another. Give the non-Western child a lollipop and he will be overjoyed, because he doesn't receive sweets very often. He is genuinely Grateful. Give the Western child the same lollipop and he may scrunch up his face because he doesn't like the flavor.

Gratitude, Generosity and Grace has already been lost. The Western child could have been happy to receive the lollipop he didn't like if he had a Generosity focus – he could give to someone else, and share in their joy.

Additionally those in 'poor' or rural communities have little to compare themselves to. Without the influence of television and media they do not focus on fame, glamour, superficial status and idealized visions of a material world – all of which promotes an *Illusionary Self focus*. There is far less SOUL pollution. They focus on what they do have rather than what others have, or what they are led to believe they 'should' have. They therefore feel more Grateful than their Western counterparts, making them 'richer' at a fundamental level. This simple differentiation provides great insight.

The enemy to Gratitude is constantly comparing your Self to others whose true circumstances you couldn't possibly know. The Truth is you are no better, no worse, no more or less valuable, than any other living being. Possessions, career and circumstances define none of us. So the act of comparing your Self simply indicates you are becoming disconnected from what really matters and *who you really are*.

See if you can re-mind your Self to simply be Grateful for what you do have, and then what you have will grow. Give and you will receive – and you do not always receive in the same way that you give. Then Graciously Love and accept others. The 3 G's feed themselves, through one another, and they feed you as well as the world you live in.

Gratitude attracts Generosity, Grace and Joy like a magnet.

Happiness cannot be traveled to, owned, earned, worn or consumed. Happiness is the spiritual experience of living every minute with love, grace and gratitude.
Denis Waitley

2.3.3   Follow Your Own Path

What makes your heart sing? Many of us have become so caught up in an Illusionary Self we no longer know the answer to that question. But it's there, hidden deep within every one of us.

As you uncover your Core Creator Self, and as you engage in and connect to only that which is Life-Generating, your heart will begin to sing again – and this time you will hear it. You may even be there already, perhaps for the first time in your life.

Ask your Self – your deepest Self – what you would do with your life if there were no limitations on possibility. Forget Illusionary

Self criteria, such as status, power or greed. What would you like to be remembered for? Is there a deep desire within you to make a difference to the world? Do you feel you would like your life to have a depth, some meaningful legacy or a profound effect on other life? Perhaps you feel inclined to live a simple life where you do what you can. Regardless, ask your Self what matters most to you. Herein you will find your inner passion.

Being part of this message, and sharing it with the world, will make your life a huge legacy in itself. You may feel inspired to run classes, workshops, discussion groups, or use your skills in creative ways to share this revelation, unite people and change the world. Even if time is limited, if you spread Life-Generating thoughts, sentiment and action, even if it's only through your conversations, you are making the world a better place. Simply ask your Self what inspires you. Then, follow that path.

See if you can stand up for what you believe in. Be a voice for the voiceless. Do and say what matters. And always honor your True Essence, which is Pure Love. Ensure everything you do comes from a place of Love, and you will engage the phenomenal.

2.3.4   Listen to Your Intuition and *Just Trust*

There is an inner knowing that comes from your Deepest Self. It is the voice of Source Energy directing you to your inner power, and to what will grow you. We call it instinct, or intuition. You may question how it differs from Brain Babble, and the answer is simple. Brain Babble is a voice of *words*. Instinct, intuition or your inner voice is a voice of *feeling*.

In fact, Brain Babble will often try to talk you out of your intuition. You may feel an illogical sense of trepidation about going somewhere or doing something, and your babble may clutter your inner knowing with reasons why you should ignore your instincts based on what you've seen, been told or been led to believe. Alternatively, you may feel a strong illogical inclination to do something or go somewhere. It's when we follow our instincts, trusting our feelings and inner knowing, that the magic happens. For instance, using a very simple example, you may sense a strong feeling to wait in a particular spot when looking for a car park, only to discover minutes or seconds later someone approaches the car by your side providing a dream parking spot.

Life will begin to flow, and literally fall into place, from the little things to the greatest things of all. And this is because you are actually communicating, at an unconscious level, with all life. You will look back in awe at what seemed like the impossible occurring – incredible synchronicity or coincidence. And this is because what has actually happened is not only are you connected to all other life at an energetic level, you've also plugged in to the ultimate power source. This is how impossible becomes *I'm-possible*. You're no longer doing it alone. You've engaged the power of the entire universe.

Extraordinary things happen when you connect to your Core Self, honour Source Energy, follow your passion and trust your inner knowing.

You see, Source Energy guides you – through your inner voice. Then as you listen and act, with Love, life unfolds in the most unbelievable ways. Proof of your connection to the Greatest Energy of All lies in the incredible coincidence, synchronicity and what we often call miracles. It's hardly surprising, as you are reconnecting with the same Source Energy that brought that egg and sperm together to create you. You are trusting and allowing *that fantastic Life Force to* take you where you need to go, in order that you truly grow. And even when it feels like you are experiencing 'bad luck' you need to trust that you will look back in hindsight and see it was actually 'good luck'.

Sam, for instance, was unable to purchase a home for his family. He, his wife Kim, and their three children, were desperate to settle down and end the continuous renting cycle they had endured for years, with ruthless landlords and often being forced to move annually. As the 'breadwinner', Sam could easily have felt like a failure. And as a person who worked tirelessly to end the people trade, Kim could have given up her generous life pursuit for a 'real job' in order to make a mortgage more easily achievable. But fortunately they both knew The Truth. They continued to hold on to their passion to do good in the world as a couple.

They reminded one another to just trust despite what seemed like pretty unfortunate experiences. Finally, their faith paid off. Sam noticed an advertised property that just seemed to call to him. Kim was reluctant to look at it, as it didn't 'tick the boxes'. But she followed his strong instinct, and that's when the magic happened. The minute Kim stepped foot into the house she was in love.

Through a series of what seemed like impossible events, one after the other, Sam and Kim found themselves the proud owners of the 'house of their dreams' the day after she viewed it for the first time. In fact, Kim had to purchase the property without Sam being able to see it in order to complete the sale in an extremely competitive market. Talk about a leap of faith. The family saw their new home the day after the sale was complete and absolutely loved it. They went out to dinner that night to celebrate, and looked back on all the properties they 'missed out' on with the deepest gratitude. "Thank God, literally!" Their children sat delightedly examining the floor plan, as Kim expressed her desire to thank the agent, Mike, for acting so scrupulously. "What about a bottle of good whiskey," suggested her mother who was with them. Somehow Kim knew Mike did not drink alcohol – at all. Somehow she also 'somehow knew' Mike had a family, despite actually knowing nothing about him. She said she'd love to buy him and his family dinner. And five minutes later, guess who approached the table? Mike and his family had felt the urge to come to the same restaurant, for the first time in their lives. It was Kim and Sam's first time too. The coincidences were out of control.

Thanks and hugs were exchanged. Mike confirmed he does not drink alcohol, and explained there were no available tables. Kim asked a passing waiter to help, and hey presto! A table was set. Kim and Sam bought Mike and his family dinner, just as they'd wished for minutes earlier.

Sam and Kim's life is full of these kinds of 'magical' experiences. They held a house-warming party, and all night their guests reported stories on incredible connection and synchronicity, with people they'd never met who lived on the other side of the city. Sam and Kim were attracting like energy, and the guests at their party were living confirmation of the greater connection they all shared.

This kind of magic can occur for you. All you need do is tune in, connect and just trust.

You are flowing and growing with and through the ultimate *Life-Generating Energy* when you trust your inner voice, follow your passions, feel your feelings, express your True Self and do it all from your Pure Love Centre.

When one door closes, another opens;
but we often look so long and so regretfully upon the closed door
that we do not see the one which has opened for us.
Alexander Graham Bell

2.3.5   Feeling Your Feelings

Part of our learning in this 'lifetime' is to experience life through a body. This means experiencing bodily functions, limitations and expressions – including feelings such as grief, anger, pain, sadness, joy, excitement, exhilaration, and a sense of Love. Our job is to accept these human experiences without judgment. We need to feel, share and express our feelings in order to grow through our lifetime. To chase our feelings away, deny them, hide them or begrudge them is to stop the engine of our body – sabotaging the purpose of this lifetime.

We are here in this realm to experience our senses. This included sight, hearing, taste, smell and touch. But we have one more sense, which we disregard as a sense, but it is the most vital of all – *our feelings*. Our feelings connect us to our inner being, and to our vitality. Our feelings connect us to the greatest connections we can make.

Feeling your feelings enables your healing. It directs you and grows you.

To deny our feelings is to deny our reason for existence. If we block the flow we are no longer able to be fully a-live in our body. If we stop being expressed, we become mechanized. If we stop being fully-sensed, we become sense-less.

When something unjust occurs and you are justifiably angry, that is constructive – provided you retain a Life-Generating focus through your feelings of anger. Your anger is there to drive you to action, and to create a more just and constructive world. If you block negative feelings, or any feelings at all, they will fester and take over you. Alternatively, if you allow your Self to feel them, they will pass through. They will come and go, driving you to constructive action in the process. So feeling your feelings enables you to turn challenges and hardships into revelations and evolution.

Think of a time when you fell over and grazed your knee badly. There was a physical pain associated with your injury. And when you felt this pain, you took note that you needed to *do something* about your injured knee. So you cleaned it, rested it and patiently allowed it to heal, knowing and accepting that you would need to take it easy for a while and that it would feel sore. Then, as a scab formed and peeled away, you finally saw the miracle of life regenerating itself as new skin was grown and your body was restored.

Now consider what would have happened if you refused to allow your Self to feel or accept the pain. You would have continued to use your knee inappropriately. You wouldn't have cleaned it so it may have become infected. You could have rejected the recovery process, picking away the scab and preventing the healing process. Your knee could have been left scarred or disfigured – as a result of you refusing to accept, appreciate and respect your feelings.

The same theory applies to all emotional pain. It's there for a reason. It needs to be felt, so it can guide, restore and ultimately protect us. Even and especially unpleasant feelings are there to take us where we need to go. But we cannot land where we need to be unless we allow our Selves to feel our feelings.

This is why the modern trend, which is becoming increasingly acceptable in our society, of handing out of psychotropic drugs or anti-depressants can be very dangerous. Mood-altering medication is the last thing we need if we are to grow and evolve through feeling our feelings. Our feelings exist for a reason – something needs to change; we need to fix or do something. When we take medication that numbs us to our emotions, or distorts our ability to feel discontent or pain, we are no longer able to resolve what needs to be resolved; we are no longer able to restore and heal. The medication acts like a band-aid, and our emotional wound festers beneath it. Therefore, we need use great caution when it comes to any form of mood-altering drugs.

They will come, and they will go. And when we allow them to guide us constructively, feelings enliven us at a deep Core level.

2.3.6   Re-Valuing "Suffering"

According to Buddhist teacher, Sri Dhammananda, our "attachment to pleasant feelings and dislike for the unpleasant ones gives rise to worry". He explains how our attempt to avoid or disassociate from the unpleasant aspects of life actually disconnects us from life itself. It makes no sense. Suffering is an unavoidable, natural part of being a fully-sensed a-live being. We need to endure battles and hardships in order to develop strength, perspective and resilience. Just as building muscles through exercise strengthens us, so do our struggles. When we shun and avoid challenges, or do all we can to evade adversity, what we fail to realize is we are simultaneously rejecting an opportunity to gain incredible strength. And Sri Dhammananda claims, our unhappiness lies, ironically, in our desire to be constantly happy.

Many of us have such a strong aversion to taking challenging action – such as leaving a destructive relationship, job or group – that we simply remain in destructive patterns that progressively deplete and destroy us. We do this for fear of facing the demands of a challenge. We fear stepping into the unknown, so instead remain in what we know regardless of how destructive it is. When we do this, when we hang on to what is not working, it's as if we are hanging on to an anchor that's preventing us from moving forward – an anchor that's sinking us.

When we are able to hold on to a Source Energy connection instead, and trust the Master Plan, which is always about creating more dynamic life and regeneration, then we would gather the strength to venture into the unknown with confidence. We would feel secure in the knowing that we are entering into no-thing, and within this no-thing anything and everything is possible.

The unknown could be anything.

Perhaps if we knew the great things that were ahead of us as we entered our most challenging battles in life, we would be overwhelmed – pressured to meet wonderful outcomes and incredible results, maybe even paralyzed by expectation. So, our strength lies in the not knowing. Through it, we are able to simply flow with the process of life, one step at a time, day by day, trusting the underlying force of all life to take us to the unimaginable. The most simple way to live is therefore the most powerful – we need to connect to the greatest Life Force of all, and our Core strength, then just trust the unfolding. This is how magnificence naturally flows to us and through us, automatically. All we need is the courage to fearlessly face the most challenging aspects of life, moment to moment.

Also we do not need to know why. When we are able to simply trust we allow the 'why' to unfold when it is ready, and when we are ready. The 'why' can be a distraction in the midst of a storm – we need to focus on surviving, on pushing through, on developing strength. So asking 'why' and looking for reasons or understanding in the depths of what we in the moment interpret as 'adversity' can cause despair or a sense of hopelessness. It connects us to the problem rather than the process of life. We are not supposed to know the reasons, yet. Our challenge lies in trusting the process of life, through our most powerful connections to Source Energy and to our Core Creator Self. Then, in hindsight we will see that the 'adversity' was a passage through to our freedom, and the reasons why could never have been known until later.

It is through the most unlikely connections that the greatest connections occur. Provided we hold onto our rudder, our Love-Directed Core Self, our challenges, 'adversity' and suffering has the capacity to take us to the greatest heights. In fact, often suffering cracks open the seed in which Pure Love lies hidden.

So our suffering keeps us alive. Just like night and day, light and dark, or sun and rain are both as necessary as the other, when we embrace both our challenging and joyous moments equally, we allow our Selves to be balanced, and to thrive. Just as without rain, nothing grows, without pain we cannot grow.

See if you can resist the temptation to avoid the 'difficult stuff'. This is like allowing your Self to only live one half of your true being. Without challenges, success cannot be experienced fully. Disabling one aspect of life disables your ability to feel another. The flow and contrast no longer exist. As symbolized in the yin yang, without one half, there is no whole.

The famous story about the kind man who watched as a butterfly struggled to emerge from its cocoon offers a memorable metaphor. The man, in an attempt to prevent suffering, cut a hole in the end of the cocoon to allow the metamorphosis to occur more easily. And then, because the butterfly was not forced to endure the battle of pushing through the darkness and breaking through the barrier, its wings had not been dried and its body had not been tapered. So it was not equipped to take flight. It was forced to sit there, unable to obtain food, unable to live. The kind man, in his attempt to prevent suffering, had unknowingly destroyed life.

The famous Buddhist lotus flower depicts this understanding. Out of the muddiest, darkest water, enlightenment grows. Manure makes great fertilizer. And just as a caterpillar emerges from the dark cocoon, reformed with wings to take flight, so too will we emerge re-formed through our suffering and most challenges times. The key is to embrace all of life.

2.3.7 Negative Thinking Sinking Sand

As much as it is imperative to embrace our suffering and challenges, it is also vitally important that we don't get caught up in them. And that is not a contradiction.

When we understand that challenges are how we grow, we grow through them. When we become attached to destruction, we will be destroyed by it.

What this means is we need to constantly watch our Brain Babble, especially during challenging times. The temptation is to begin a cycle of thinking that is destructive. And if we connect to, focus on, and build that, we become diminished, and detached from life.

Even when we are facing our biggest 'problems' or challenges, we need to remain SOUL-focused and Love-directed. If we allow our Selves to start focusing on the problem itself, then we risk sinking into Negative Thinking Sinking Sand. And it can happen quite subliminally, especially when we are under pressure or overwhelmed. So we need to keep our Selves awake and aware, especially when we are facing trials.

When we feel like we are immersed in our problems, we can fall into the trap of thinking we are our problems. Then we forget *who we really are*. And we lose our power. The more immersed in Negative

Thinking Sinking Sand we become, the harder it becomes to escape it. A bit like quicksand, we pull others in to our sinking pit rather than allow them to pull us out.

For this reason, it is important to understand that if you become trapped in Negative Thinking Sinking Sand, the only way out is to change your Brain Babble – or what you allow your Self to focus on or believe. Your babble can sink you. And when that happens it is very difficult for others to rescue you.

This is why, as well intentioned as you may be, it can be dangerous to try to rescue those deep in Negative Thinking Sinking Sand, as it is likely you will be dragged under with them. Just as the kind man tried to 'help' the butterfly escape the cocoon in vain, we can do more damage than good by trying to rescue others sometimes.

No one saves us but ourselves. No one can and no one may. We ourselves must walk the path.
Buddha

This doesn't mean we stand by and watch another's suffering or tribulation heartlessly. Quite the contrary. Share this message, or any other that you feel will help awaken others. Extend a Loving hand of friendship and companionship – without allowing your Self to get caught up in repetitive Negative Thinking. Step away from engaging in destructive patterns of thinking, speaking or behaving, with Love. And see if you are able to be a constant reminder to others of their Inner Essence, their True Self, their power and their strength.

So if someone you know or care about whines constantly about their problems or behaves in destructive ways, offer them a Life-Generating, Love-Centered focus. Then, if they refuse to hear you and continue to remain attached to their problem, offer it again. Direct them to a book or message that will help them like this one. Finally, if they are unable to hear you, step away with Love. And then go back when you feel the time is right, to reiterate a Life-Generating focus. Be sure to let others know that you are there for them, and you will do all you can to enable and grow them, as long as they want to grow them Selves. Hang on to the 3 G's and remain SOUL-focused. This is the most encouraging and Loving thing you can do.

When we focus on 'a problem', or something we perceive as 'negative', we become part of that thinking, or babble. Then we are feeding and growing the problem, and we have become part of it. We have become enmeshed in it.

Remember, what you focus on grows. So the Energy of the problem then begins to take over your Energy. Toxic 'thoughts' act like magnets for destruction. Then, before you know it, you find your

Self making damaging connections, descending you into a deep bottomless pit.

Don't forget: you are *not* your thoughts. Thoughts are simply a mechanism of your brain or mind. By thinking you are your thinking you are surrendering your Authentic Self completely to your Illusionary Self. Additionally, you are also the opposite to 'negative'. You are Love-Directed Life-Generating unlimited Energy. So to get caught up in Negative Thinking is to lose touch with everything you actually are.

In saying this, thoughts are the most powerful navigation tool or steering wheel you have. You need to choose them carefully. And if you find your Self spiraling into this dreadful pit, remember you are just a choice away from your freedom – a thought choice. The minute you are able to recognize the fact that your thinking is twisting you down a negative spiral, you are ninety percent of the way to changing your thinking. From there it's simply a matter of re-minding your Self, to break a bad habit.

Awareness is your savior. To escape anything, we must first know we are in it.

Think of a moth, flying in aimless circles around a light, unable to escape a dreaded fate. His focus is killing him, because he is unaware of how destructive his focus is. Unlike the moth, awareness and a determined focus will redirect us to life.

Notice your Brain Babble. Do you criticize others, feel badly done by, or misunderstood? Are you pessimistic, or harsh in your judgment of your Self and others? Do you notice faults before virtues? Can you feel resentment, anger and bitterness growing? Or do you see the good, the silver lining, the light at the end of the tunnel? Do you face your challenges with strength and determination, or do you feel victimized by them? See if you can be honest about your Babble and the way in which you are allowing it to direct you.

If your inner focus is not Life-Generating, choose a different inner focus – one that will enrich and expand your Love-focused Essence. There is no right or wrong, other than that.

The ultimate value of life depends upon awareness and the power of contemplation rather than upon mere survival.
Aristotle

2.3.8   Expectation = Limitation

When we expect an outcome, we reject the creative process of life. We disconnect from limitless possibility. Our expectations become our limitations. This is because our current expectations are based on our current conscious knowing. If, however, we are connected to the Greatest Life Source of all Creation, then we cannot even imagine the outcome. Often, in fact usually, it will surpass all our expectations. So to turn impossibility into I'm-possibility, we need to hold on to our Core Self, focus on what grows all life, do all we can to create and generate the *I'm-possible*, trust, and then watch what unfolds.

It's fine to have goals, so long as you allow your goals to change, evolve and grow with life as it unfolds around you. Perceived 'failure' is an illusion, and it feeds your Illusionary Self. It disconnects you from your power. It paralyses and stagnates you. And all failure is borne out of expectation.

Expectation diminishes creation. It stifles inspiration. It fuels limitation.

Next time you find your Self expecting or anticipating a specific result or outcome, or being disappointed that life hasn't turned out the way you expected it to, see if you are able to let your expectations go. Then Graciously and Gratefully accept what happens and what has happened. Acceptance frees you to Open your Self up to what is new, and emerging. Expectation closes you down and shuts out possibility. So focus on remaining SOUL-

THE TRUTH AD INFINITUM

THE TRUTH AD INFINITUM

directed, regardless of the direction your life takes. Simply expect life to surprise you – magnificently – and it will, even if the steps to that magnificence are not the steps you would have chosen to take.

2.3.9   Rejection = Redirection

There is not such thing as rejection when you are Love-focused, Source-directed and connected to your Core Self.

Any perceived 'rejection' is simply a re-direction away from what is depleting you, or towards what you need to be fulfilled and on track.

When we 'lose' something or someone, we gain Empty Space – which will be filled with something more aligned and synchronized. To let go Graciously, and even Gratefully, re-connects us to a re-generative flow.

Turn your face to the sun and the shadows fall behind you.
Maori proverb

Even when you feel like the person, opportunity or privilege you 'lost' was Life-Generating, you will eventually be able to see in hindsight that it was in fact a distraction, trap, or time-consuming mis-direction in disguise. It may take months or years to gain this perspective, but it will happen. And that is guaranteed when you are Source-directed. So remind your Self to *just trust*.

Source Energy is all-knowing, and all-encompassing, as we are all essentially part of it. Every babble pattern, directive, focus, incentive or agenda holds energy, which Source Energy recognizes – and which you or I often don't. We are embodied and in many ways limited to our senses as part of this life experience, although we now know this dimension does not define *who we really are*. However, when we are connected to Source Energy, we plug back in to that multi-sensory, multi-dimensional and entirely unlimited Essence of *who we really are*, and of life itself. So we tap into that infinite possibility, without necessarily sensing it through our current mode of sensory perception. So then we become channeled, directed and re-directed in brilliant ways that we, in our current realm of existence, may not understand or comprehend logically. This process therefore requires what we call 'trust'. We are handing over to the greatest life force of all, trusting our instincts, acting SOUL-fully and knowing that whatever unfolds will be exactly what it should be.

When you know you are connected to goodness, and all that generates all life, you can be absolutely certain that whatever and whoever comes your way, and whatever and whoever parts ways with you, did so for a very good reason – even if you cannot 'see' it.

THE TRUTH AD INFINITUM

This does not mean that your perceived loss will not feel sad, or painful. In fact, feeling your feelings enables your healing. And in order to make room for someone or something much more empowering to you, you need to first heal and gather your Self. Once you have gone through the healing process, through feeling your feelings, you will be free to look back with Gratitude rather than regret as you walk your new path.

2.3.10 The Failure Illusion

'Failure' connects us to expectation and rejection, both of which disconnect us from the greatest creative processes of life. So 'failure' is non-sense.

We learn, grow and evolve through our experiences. Each perceived 'success' or 'gain' is as valuable as each considered 'failure', 'loss', or 'burden' because life is not about 'success'; it is in itself a *passage through* – an em-bodied, *zoning in* to the smaller details of sensory *be-in-g*.

All 'failure' is associated with an expected outcome that was not achieved. But often, the expected outcome is in fact an unrecognized limitation.

Antje, for example, really struggled at schoolwork and often disrupted the class with her constant fidgeting and restlessness. At 10 years of age, she had achieved none of the expected results and achievements for her age in science, math, history or English. Her mother took Antje to a specialist to find out what was 'wrong' with her. The secretary had left for the day and Antje waited alone in the waiting room. After a long discussion, the specialist returned with the mother to find Antje waving her arms around almost uncontrollably to the music she was listening to through her earphones. Her eyes were shut. She was in a world of her own.

"She obviously loves music," the specialist observed.

"Oh yes!" Antje's mother exclaimed. "And she's a brilliant pianist."

The specialist was a wise man, and he turned to Antje's mother with a gentle smile, "Antje is a musician. Put her into a music school and forget about the other subjects. See what happens."

Antje's mother followed the advice and Antje joined a school for musically gifted children. She flourished and felt, at last, that she fitted in with her peers. They were all as 'mad' as her!

Antje went on to become an internationally acclaimed composer and her beautiful musical masterpieces are themes to some of the most famous and emotionally charged movies of our times. She lives her passion, and is a great 'success', but her 'success' was actually driven from a perceived 'failure'. She often looks back with wonder, awe and the absolute Gratitude for the challenges she faced through her early childhood years in the traditional school system. And also for the SOUL-focused wisdom and courage of two people who could have made her or broken her – her mother and that very intuitive specialist. Many other adults may have chosen a course of ADHD medication, numbed her response to life, and dismissed her as 'abnormal'.

Sometimes what we perceive as failure is actually the beginning of the greatest success.

Whether our experiences are desired at the time or not, they re-form and reform us if we are able to move on and flow with them and through them.

So when we are able to embrace perceived 'failure' with as much Gratitude as perceived 'success', both words lose their meaning – and we re-connect to living life meaningfully. With a SOUL-full focus, we will blossom in miraculous ways – and we will eventually look back and see our times of scarcity as a process of seeding.

See if you can allow your Self to flow, accepting what comes your way as well as what does not. See if you are able to appreciate what is, what was, what will be, and what isn't, equally. Then watch your Spontaneous Open Uninhibited Loving Self grow you in unimaginable ways.

I have woven a parachute out of everything broken.
William Stafford

2.3.11 Weeding

We cannot connect to certain things unless we dis-connect from others.

The Truth is we cannot focus on joy and bitterness at the same time. We cannot love while full of hatred. And for this reason, we cannot heal while seeking revenge.

Like weeds in the garden of your SOUL, any destructive connections to people, organizations, practices or anything at all, will dis-able the growth of Life-Generating connections. As you plant new seedlings, and feed them with Love, you need to remove any weeds to make space for the regenerative life to grow.

When you remove destructive connections, you are weeding. This enables your Essence to re-seed.

Try to be as honest as you can. Look at all your connections, and try to see them with an open mind regardless of who or what they are, how long they've been around and how much a part of your current life they've become. Try to simplify what they are doing to you, for you, and with you. If they are constructive, Life-Generating and grow you, then embrace them. And if they are destructive or Life-Depleting to you or others, then now is the time to let them go – with Love, Grace, Gratitude, acceptance and peace.

Realize that no letting go is permanent. Life is an ever-unfolding process. And when you let something or someone go, with Love, you are setting both your Self and them free. Your SOUL Self will always be there for that person or situation to return, when the connection is Love-directed and constructive.

Remember, you can never 'lose' anything, or anyone. You are eternally and beautifully connected to everything and everyone at the deepest level. None of us own or have anything. Permanence is a delusion, as is end and beginning. All life is a collective stream, in which we each flow and grow. Even if you need to let your destructive parents go for a little while, in order make space for a regenerative, revitalized life, you have not lost your family. You have simply disconnected from actions that deplete you. Your Love connection is an inner Energetic connection, and this will continue and remain.

When you enable destructive behavior, especially when it is directed at you, you are fueling destruction, and dis-abling your Self as well as those projecting the destruction onto you. There is nothing Life-Generating about that. Often we do it in the name of 'love' but real Love fuels only that which is constructive and Life-Generating. If you are able to make it clear to those whose behavior is destructive that you Love them, and would like to re-connect with them at a personal level when their actions support this Love, you are actually empowering both your Self and them.

To be who you were born to be requires a resolute Love-directed determined strength.

You must not lose faith in humanity.
Humanity is an ocean;
if a few drops of the ocean are dirty, the ocean does not become dirty.
Gandhi

2.4

Where to From Here

We move on to the next part of this Condensed Version of The Truth with many of the fundamental tools required to take this revolutionary way of *be-in-g* into the world.

Armed with a simplified new language, which we are forming together, we have become well and truly united in our quest for a new direction and a new world. It is you and I, the people of the world, who hold the power to change it. And despite what we are led to believe, regardless of the brainwashing and propaganda we receive, this is The Truth.

As we move on together, we will uncover some of the techniques used to keep us in our powerless Illusionary Self state. And it's very simple. Once we can see The Truth we will never be blinded again.

Gandhi offers us a wonderfully powerful example of how to enable magnificence. Regardless of whether he was jailed, mocked, ridiculed or mistrusted, he continued to hold on to a SOUL focus. He practiced resolute Love, peace and retained a Life-Generating focus. He embraced suffering and challenges with Truth, integrity and Love. He showed us how, out of what appeared to be the impossible dream, *I'm-possibility* became a reality.

Under oppressed British Colonial rule, India became independent and free, and although we give Gandhi credit for this, the true power lay in those who followed his lead. As others took on the plight for freedom, through a dedication to peace, non-violent resistance to destruction, and a Life-Generating focus, the power of the people overthrew what was destroying them. Martin Luther King followed Gandhi's lead, changing the world. And we can do the same.

If we unite in this message, one by one, with a determined and unshakable focus, we will transform the world we live in. It's not an idealistic dream. It's a reality. And it begins with you. Thank you for changing the world.

Everybody can be great because anybody can serve.
You don't have to have a college degree to serve.
You don't have to make your subject and verb agree to serve.
You only need a heart full of grace. A soul generated by love.
Martin Luther King Jr.

Author's Note

You are a Revolutionist

Simply by reading and becoming part of this message,
you are a Revolutionist.
You have become part of the most magnificent Life Force available to mankind.
It is through you that we will transcend the world we live in,
now and forever.
Thank you for engaging in the only thing that matters.
Thank you for trusting your instincts,
listening to your intuition,
hearing your inner SOUL voice,
without which you would not be part of this revolutionary path.

You were already connected.
You were a part of this vital movement
before you found this message,
which is why you discovered it.

Thank you
for being the magnificent inter-connected Limitless Energy you are.
You are extraordinary beyond words.
You exceed your own imagination,
and this is why what you are unfolding
through the process of embracing and living this message,
will be inconceivably astounding.

Thank you for spreading the word.
Thank you for doing all you can
to make this dream a reality
that will change reality for all, always.

You are creating a new future for your children,
for our children,
and for their grandchildren.
You are living your life in the most powerful way you can.

I honor your Generous, pure SOUL.
Without you
this message cannot do what it needs to do.

THE TRUTH AD INFINITUM

Thank you
for changing the world.
Yours with the greatest humility and Love,

AD Infinitum

Desiderata

Go placidly amidst the noise and haste,
and remember what peace there may be in silence.
As far as possible without surrender
be on good terms with all persons.
Speak your truth quietly and clearly;
and listen to others,
even the dull and the ignorant; they too have their story.
Avoid loud and aggressive persons,
they are vexatious to the spirit.
If you compare yourself with others,
you may become vain or bitter;
for always there will be greater and lesser persons than yourself.
Enjoy your achievements as well as your plans.
Keep interested in your own career, however humble;
it is a real possession in the changing fortunes of time.
Exercise caution in your business affairs;
for the world is full of trickery.
But let this not blind you to what virtue there is;
many persons strive for high ideals;
and everywhere life is full of heroism.
Be yourself.
Especially, do not feign affection.
Neither be cynical about love;
for in the face of all aridity and disenchantment
it is as perennial as the grass.
Take kindly the counsel of the years,
gracefully surrendering the things of youth.
Nurture strength of spirit to shield you in sudden misfortune.
But do not distress yourself with dark imaginings.
Many fears are born of fatigue and loneliness.
Beyond a wholesome discipline, be gentle with yourself.
You are a child of the universe,
no less than the trees and the stars; you have a right to be here.
And whether or not it is clear to you,
no doubt the universe is unfolding as it should.
Therefore be at peace with God, whatever you conceive Him to be,
and whatever your labors and aspirations,
in the noisy confusion of life keep peace with your soul.
With all its sham, drudgery, and broken dreams,

THE TRUTH AD INFINITUM

it is still a beautiful world.
Be cheerful.
Strive to be happy.

Max Ehrmann

Part Three:

Welcome to the Revolution

Starting Thoughts

Now you are connected to your vitality,

you are again united with your True Essence,

the Energy of ALL life

and the greatest power of all.

You will start to see unthinkable magnificence unfold in your life

and all around you.

And as you see and react to the world differently,

it will begin to change before your eyes.

The hope of a secure and livable world
lies with disciplined nonconformists,
who are dedicated to justice, peace, and brotherhood.
The trailblazers in human, academic, scientific, and religious freedom
have always been nonconformists.
In any cause that concerns the progress of mankind,
put your faith in the nonconformist!

Martin Luther King Jr.

3.0

Part Three

Creating a New World

You are now ready to emerge, from the sanctity of your cocoon, into the world around you. You are not the same. You are forever changed. There is no going back. The only certainty is you will one day look back in awe as to where this awakening has taken you. It will be beyond your imagination. It will reflect *I'm-possibility*. All you need to do from here is hold on, tightly, to *who you really are*, and to the new connections you have made – the most powerful connections of all.

The truth is you have everything you need. Through your connection to the Greatest Life Force on Earth, you can face even the most overwhelming realities with confidence to change and evolve them in mind-boggling ways. If you hold on to the Energy of

All Life, what unfolds will be as marvelous as a newborn child – undreamed of, beautiful, unique and exquisitely miraculous.

Remember though, to emerge into a new realm of reality must involve a challenge. Just as the butterfly requires strength and determination to break through the cocoon wall and discover the wings he never knew he had, you too will require strength and determination in order to break away from the worldly trappings that keep you stuck and confined.

We cannot change the world without some struggle, just as Mahatma Gandhi, Martin Luther King and Nelson Mandela could not have liberated the world without a *plight* for freedom. But this challenge is the greatest challenge of all; it is the only challenge that matters – we are claiming our own survival, and our ability to thrive, as individuals, and as a human race. It represents our ultimate life purpose, and our united *passage through* to freedom and peace. And it affects our children's future more than anything else we can do for them or give them.

This is the challenge of our time. And it is time, now, to face our ultimate challenge, individually and collectively.
To not face this challenge would ironically be much more challenging. If we continue to walk the path we are on, independently and as a whole we will self-destruct. And it will

happen insidiously. By the time we realize it is happening it will be too late.

It is important that we do not act out of fear though. Fear apposes *who we really are* – which is Love. Because we have all been so blinded to our power and Essence, for so very long, we had simply become lost. There in nothing to fear once we know are all part of the elemental and fundamental Life Force, connected to one another in the most profound ways. You and I are infinitely powerful, but unite us at a Source level and our power is catapulted in ways we could never conceive or comprehend. Do that a million times over, and over, and then we will literally all be mind blown by what we have enabled and created.

Freedom awaits you. It awaits us all. We simply need to choose it. We need to link arms and make new choices in order to determine a new direction.

As you look around you now, with foggy goggles no longer distorting your vision, the world and its influence, its trappings, will become increasingly clear. You will 'see' everything in a whole new way. You will literally see the truth through your awakening. And you will begin to be naturally discerning, protecting your Core Self and harnessing your phenomenal strength. You will know what's right. You will know what matters. And then you will say, do and be the change. You are the change this world needs. You, and me, and anyone willing to see, will create a new reality.

This movement may begin as an undercurrent, a subtle driving force. And then, as the truth spreads, awakening more and more people, before we know it, it will become a tidal wave. As Malcolm Gladwell (2002) explains in his book *The Tipping Point*, ideas and messages spread like viruses. And this is one 'virus' the world desperately needs to survive.

We are forming the most exciting evolution mankind has ever seen. We are generating and creating the most remarkable history on our planet, and evolving a new future. This is fantastic. We are changing what doesn't work, and making it work. There is nothing more marvelous than that. And this section takes us through the steps and pitfalls. It shows us how to change our world, as one and as all, for once and for all.

Let's do it!

Do not conform any longer to the pattern of this world,
but be transformed by the renewing of your mind.
Romans 12:2 NIV

3.1

Current Reality

The truth is parts of our current reality are stifling, derailing and even destroying us – and we are oblivious to it. They are distracting us from *who we really are*, making it impossible for us to live our purpose and experience a fulfilled life. The problem is many of these aspects of our reality have become a way of being for us – a habit. We have existed continually in a particular, repetitive cycle – and therefore we have begun to normalize ways of being that disconnect us from our vitality, and from everything that truly matters. And when we have lost our connection to what matters, we can no longer see what matters. We can no longer be what matters. Then we become like that moth, flying aimlessly on autopilot around in circles, fixated on a delusive light that is in fact a treacherous trap.

Our bodies will break down under the pressure of living an unnatural existence like this, just as wild animals rarely thrive in captivity. We see proof of this in the growing number of mental and physical health issues. When we lose our Core Selves we are completely lost. We feel empty. And this makes us even more susceptible to that which sickens us.

This section outlines how and why parts of our society and surrounding world render us lost, trapped and powerless. It shows us how to reclaim our Essence in the face of our current reality, and how to evolve, revive and reconfigure the world around us in order for us to thrive and generate magnificence.

To change anything we must first see it for what it is.

Here, we do just that. We see the world for what it is. And that allows us to transcend it rather than be bogged down in it. Then the world will catch up, with us. Here, we forge a new path together. And we can rest assured that the world will follow, because every one of us knows, deep down, that this is the only way forward.

The most damaging phrase in the language is:
"It's always been done that way".
Grace Murray Hopper

3.1.1 Disconnecting

Now it is time to take a good hard look at the connections you have made, and decide which are Constructive and which are Destructive. It is important to understand that if you are allowing others to act in harmful and hurtful ways, you are allowing them to be a Destructive force in the world – and they are not just Destructive to those whom they direct harm, but to themselves, and to the Energy of which we are all part. So, what this means is you are acting with complete Love if you peacefully walk away from Destructive action, regardless of where it's coming from. You are also preserving all life by refusing to be part of any damaging activity or behavior, and by doing all you can to stop it peacefully but determinedly.

So give your Self permission to walk away from all Destructive patterns, regardless of who or what they are, and no matter how long or closely you've been connected to them or associated with them. We cannot be SOUL Directed and create a new Love centered movement while we are allowing others to act in Life Depleting ways towards us, or while we are part of destructive groups and associations. We cannot connect to and engage in the ultimate Powerful Omnipresent Life Source while we are also connected to and engaged in division or judgment. It really is not complicated. The problem is we, through generations of Imposed and Foundational Connections, have made the simplest facts ridiculously complicated – to the point where we have lost the message and we no longer know what really matters.

What you connect to is crucial. And what you disconnect from is just as crucial. If it, they, or them, are Life Generating and Love Directed, connect. If not, disconnect. That is all that matters.

157

You have now become part of the most powerful Life Generating Force on earth. And what matters most is to stay connected through a complete SOUL-full focus. Be absolutely determined. And allow nothing and no one to deter you. Choose your friends very carefully. And be meticulously selective and discerning about the groups you engage in and connect to.

Resist the temptation to engage in a fight. There is no need to convince those who are not interested in changing to change. The most powerful thing we can do is take responsibility for our *own action*, be Open about what we are doing and why, and then allow others the process of their own unfolding, without judgment. Just as trying to change your Brain Babble engages it, and grows it, simply through focusing on it, the same thing happens when you try to change people or wrestle those who are caught up in Destructive patterns of behavior. Like Negative Thinking Sinking Sand, to do so will take you under. Simply walk away, with Love – and send them a copy of The Truth. They will join the revolution when they are ready.

You are free now. And your choices will keep you connected to and part of the greatest unfolding of freedom you could ever imagine.

Self-realization means that we have been consciously connected with our source of being. Once we have made this connection, then nothing can go wrong.
Swami Paramananda

3.1.2 Collective Energy

When a group of people comes together through a united and determined focus, a *Collective Energy* is automatically formed. We see this in numerous community congregations including religious, political, corporate and recreational group gatherings. Consider a rock concerts, for example. People gather together to enjoy a shared music experience, one they collectively enjoy. Through that commonality, and a focal point being the performer, the crowd create a powerful Collective Energy, which can be intense, exciting and intoxicating. This can also be experienced in churches, particularly evangelical churches, where people are encouraged to express themselves and share enthusiasm for their faith. Usually encouraged by a leader, the focus and expression literally becomes contagious, and eventually the entire group seems to be behaving in a type of orchestrated way. They resemble one another, generating Energy from and through those around them. As we know, what you focus on grows. So when you have a large group who unite in a common focus, the Energy generated through that focus grows *exponentially*.

The larger the group, the more powerful the Collective Energy is likely to be. And the more palpable and infectious it will become. Usually a Collective Energy will start with one person, or a small focus group, who set an example. Then, one by one, the rest of the group follows.

> *There is a fascinating YouTube video uploaded by Derek Sivers (2010) that illustrates this beautifully. A group of people are filmed sitting in a park, and suddenly one person begins to dance freely. At this point he is an outsider to the group – perhaps a 'freak' or 'weirdo'. Then, one other person joins him. This person actually had the courage to turn the lone dancer into a potential movement. Then, a second person joined in, and this became the tipping point if you like. No verbal communication occurred. And suddenly, at a very fast pace, others began to join in the fun. When the second person joined the dancing group, the potential movement became a reality, which is why the greatest leaders are actually the first committed followers of an original or new idea.*

Collective Energy, like all Energy, is either Life Generating or Life Depleting; and either way it holds much greater power than Individual Energy alone.

Because Collective Energy is an accumulation of mass Individual Energy, it is much more powerful than non-united Individual Energy, and therefore it can drive its focus very fast. If that focus is

Source-directed, it will engage in the ultimate creative genius; the dynamic manifestation of Life itself.

Clearly, dancing and having fun, connecting to others in a friendly way, and embracing those around you as one or as an equal is a SOUL-full expression of life. On a much larger scale, there have been historical examples of the power of Collective Energy at work. Virtually every Love-directed religious or even political leader illustrated powerfully Life-Generating Collective Energy. Mother Teresa, Gandhi, Martin Luther King, for example, showed us how when we engage with others through a Life-Generating focus, and this focus is shared, one by one our Individual Energy combines to create an incredible result. Destructive systems can be peacefully overthrown. Divided people can be united. The accepted status quo is permanently altered. What appeared to be impossible becomes *I'm-possible*.

If we did the things we were capable of doing,
we would literally astound ourselves.
Thomas Edison

3.1.3 Expansionary Energy

On the other hand, there are unfortunately horrific examples of Destructive Collective Energy at work as well. The obvious historical example is Hitler's Germany. An insane, deadly Collective Energy turned people into facilitators of atrocity through a forced attachment to, and promotion of, division, fear and hatred. The Collective Energy grew, exponentially, but without a Source-directed focus. And that grew catastrophe.

A Collective Energy that is not Source directed also grows at an increasingly rapid rate, as more people join in or support the thought process, movement or belief system. Because what we focus on grows, when a large group of people promote and share a Destructive focus, the resulting Collective Energy will attract a great expansion as the group gains numbers and momentum. This energy is called *Expansionary Energy*. It generates growth, but Destructive growth because it is not Source directed. And this is how all the most devastating forces on earth take hold.

In contrast to Source Energy, which can grow anything out of no-thing, Expansionary Energy can only be a catalyst to what is already growing. Source Energy and Expansionary Energy therefore combine to generate magnificence when the focus is Life-Generating. However, when the focus is Life-Depleting, Expansionary Energy acts alone.

What this means is Collective Energy is always much stronger than Individual Energy, but if the Collective Energy is Source directed it will overthrow a Collective Energy that is not Source directed.

Source directed Collective Energy is infinitely more powerful than Destructive Collective Energy, because it carries with it the ultimate Life Force.

We can be deeply encouraged by this knowing, as what it tells us is provided we remain committed and attached to a Constructive Source Directed Collective Energy we can and will overpower and conquer any Destructive Collective Energy. The secret lies in numbers. Although a Constructive Collective Energy requires a smaller number of people to hold the same power as Destructive Collective Energy, its ultimate strength grows with the number of supporters, advocates and campaigners or enthusiastic 'cheerleaders' in its midst. As more of us join a Constructive Movement, momentum will grow and the power of the movement will multiply at an incredible pace because it will be driven by the Source of Life itself.

We can overcome all Destruction on earth provided we unite in a Constructive Collective Energy.

Hatred does not cease by hatred, but only by love; this is the eternal rule.
Buddha

Take a look for a moment at Apartheid South Africa. How could a 7 percent minority exploit and subjugate a 93 percent majority? Well the answer is very simple. The 93 percent minority were divided. The 'black' community of South Africa consisted of many tribes who were at loggerheads. Their lack of unity, or inability to form a united Life-Generating Collective Energy, allowed a small minority to crush and enslave them to the extreme through propaganda, manipulation and suppression.

Unless we unite though a Source Directed Collective Energy as a human race, we too are at grave risk of being controlled, crushed and subjugated by a powerful minority.

The truth is the most effective way to control and disempower any group is to divide them amongst themselves. And the most effective way to empower, liberate and free any group is to unite them.

Step outside of these words for a few minutes, and look at the Collective Energy that is being formed in our current world. Consider for example the "War on Terrorism", or the "Freedom Fighters" who represent violent extremist groups. Powerful Collective Energy is forming through these campaigns. But ask your Self, your Core Self, honestly, are they creating a Constructive or

Destructive Collective Energy force. Surely a "war" or "fight" is Destructive, regardless of how you look at it. But to have a war against a revolutionary, a radical or an anarchist – who could be anyone, including you or I – well surely that has to be one of the most oppressive and Destructive Collective Energy forces ever created. Every great revolutionary leader who ever walked this earth could now be labeled a "terrorist". New laws and regulations have been passed that allow governments and authorities to arrest, torture and imprison anyone without trial, for any period of time. In this current world reality, Gandhi, Mandela, Jesus, Muhammad, Mother Teresa, Martin Luther King and all the greatest people who ever lived could have been apprehended indefinitely, and legally. This "War on Terrorism" is dangerously ambiguous. It could be the final war against the freedom of mankind. But we can stop it. What we need to do is refuse to attach to it, or believe it. Then we need to unite and stand up against it.

How can you have a war on terrorism when war itself is terrorism?
Howard Zinn

We need to be as cautious as possible with regard to the Collective Energy we support, connect to, accept and become a part of. If it is SOUL-full, Love-centered and Source directed, it will grow unthinkable magnificence. If it is Destructive, especially today in a world where we are interconnected in ways we could never have dreamed of even decades ago, we could be connecting to and growing what will become our complete demise.

Remember, we are all part of one another at the most profound and fundamental level, so to engage in anything that is Destructive to another will ultimately destroy you, and everyone else.

We may believe we have no choice or control. But that's where we are deluded. We actually have all the control. No one can form a group, or a Collective Energy, without supporters or followers.

Think back to our lone dancer. Should no one have joined him, the movement would never have occurred. If we all refused to fire a bullet, no one would get shot. If no one joined the army, there would be no war. If we stopped buying misery, it would not exist. If we boycotted any organization or company that engaged in unscrupulous, ruthless, cruel or exploitative activity, we would drive ethical business. If we all refused to violate others there would be no violence. If we saw the "War on Terrorism" as an imposed and Destructive propaganda tool, which promotes optimal fear and division amongst all of us, while giving a small minority the ultimate power to subdue, suppress and detain or demolish anyone or anything for no real reason, then we would rise up against it. We would see it for the Destructive non-sense it really is. And the minority who are promoting it would no longer hold the power. There is no way they could arrest or detain the entire population.

We must stand together, united, not as nations, not as countries, but as a human race.

An eye for an eye will only make the whole world blind.
Mahatma Gandhi

3.1.4   Subliminal Connections

When we are in an Illusionary Self state, we become part of what surrounds us, unknowingly. In this state we have no Core Strength to hold on to, no rudder, no real directive, so we unintentionally and unwittingly become shaped and governed by life around us. These connections are called *Subliminal Connections*, because they take hold of us unconsciously, especially when we are unaware of *who we really are*.

Every day, without our conscious awareness, Subliminal Connections manipulate, persuade, influence and control us in powerful ways, many of which are Destructive to us. And this is because when we are lost to our Illusionary Self, we don't recognize what is Destructive to us. Trends, patterns, acceptable ways of 'thinking' and behaving, media, social media, technology, music, movies, books, magazines, entertainment, video games, 'news' and advertising are commonly used to create a particular 'norm' for 'all', or 'norm-all'. Once people normalize and accept something, they are unlikely to see it as a problem even if it is one.

Subliminal Connections can therefore be very deceptive. They can be 'sold' or promoted as good for us when in fact they are quite the opposite. They can appear innocuous, or even Constructive, when really they are carefully camouflaged traps.

Beware of false knowledge; it is more dangerous than ignorance.
George Bernard Shaw

The good news is when we have awoken to the truth, and when we know what feeds our Core Self, we are much less likely to be deceived. Destructive Subliminal Connections suddenly become clearly visible to us, and we can then easily and consciously avoid them.

Lets take for example, the current trend in the popular music industry. Have you noticed that there seem to be a very small handful of recording artists whose songs are played repeatedly on the radio, to the point where most of us are screaming for something different? Do you think it's a coincidence that most of these popular artists promote a similar message through their music? Generally, it's a sex, drugs or a self-value Illusionary Self focus and culture.

Historically it hasn't been this way. Musicians have been the voice of awakening, the voice of reason, often being forerunners in a revolutionary focus uniting and strengthening people with hope. They have provided a voice for change, for goodness, for integration, or even a radical shift in sentiment. Think back only a few years ago, to Cat Steven's "Peace Train" or John Lennon's "Imagine". The music industry was full of revolutionary peace seekers who generated a Source Directed Collective Energy. Where are these types of musicians now? Well, they still exist, in the millions. But the minority, who control the mainstream media, are not allowing them to be heard. Instead, what they allow us to hear, repeatedly, sends us a message of hedonism, extravagance, escapism through drugs or unattached sex, or simple meaninglessness – and this creates a 'norm-all' that actually divides us rather than unites us. Occasionally a SOUL-full song will manage to creep into the 'mainstream' but usually these artists will have a short lived exposure to the 'masses' – unless they change their focus to one which fits the current 'norm'.

The same thing happens in the movie industry. Do you think it's a coincidence that the movies we are exposed to are becoming increasingly violent? Have you wondered how explicit, sense-less sex has become normalized and emotional attachment at a deep level is the exception rather than the rule? What about the ratings? How come what was rated "M" for Mature Audiences is now being rated

"PG" or even "G" normalizing SOUL-less, Life Depleting examples for our children.

Setting an example is not the main means of influencing others;
it is the only means.
Albert Einstein

The fact is we have the ultimate choice.   No one can force us to watch movies where killing is a game or sport for example, or where explicit, exploitative and abusive sex is attractive.   Once we see how Destructive this type of "entertainment" is to *who we really are*, we will simply refuse to buy it.   We will not expose our children to it. We will see this type of entertainment for exactly what it is – a powerful way to disconnect us from our ultimate strength, rendering us powerless and connected to what destroys us at an essence-ial level.

When we make this choice, the movie "industry" will have to change.   If we refuse to buy what is Destructive to us there will be no more box office successes out of this kind of material.   The industry will have to evolve with us.   They will have to create movies that feed us.   Or perhaps we will need to create a company that produces movies that generate a Constructive Collective Energy – and a new Life Generating 'norm-all'.

The point is we hold the power.

The truth is we can be magnificently propelled and supported, or dreadfully hindered and hijacked, by that which we often barely notice.

As you watch the news now, you will notice the reality. You will see that mainstream news directs our focus with a corporate and political agenda. We may be encouraged to focus on a local tragedy to distract us from the war we are engaged in and from the thousands of lives our government destroys in other countries for political gain. Our attention may be diverted to menial celebrity stories to deflect our focus away from major global issues. Perhaps we will be directed to the price of groceries to distract us from focusing on the fact that we are facilitating horrific cruelty and suffering through our live animal export trade.

Much of the time mainstream news stories promote a political and commercial agenda. Therefore we can actually be mis-informed through them. Any news that arouses fear, aggression and division, such as the current terrorism focus, are Destructive to the extreme. There are plenty of non-mainstream news sites that provide unbiased information. We do not need to accept the current mainstream. And the fact is, when we change what we accept, what is acceptable will change.

If you don't read the newspaper, you're uninformed.
If you do read the newspaper, you're mis-informed.
Mark Twain

In the same way we can choose the games, movies, books, internet sites, and social media sites we connect to. We can download music that feeds our SOUL and support musicians that unite us, empower us, provide us with a voice of reason, and a new way forward. Then that will grow and our world will automatically change.

We hold the power, you and I. And once we know that we will create the world we all want and need.

We need to know that when we support or connect to anything that glorifies or promotes violence, self indulgence, decadence, abusive or exploitative sex, division, control, oppression, marginalization or segregation we are Depleting all life, at every level, especially our own. And we are sabotaging our children's future.

So when it comes to social media for example, we can simply adjust what we connect to. We can block news feeds that are Destructive, narcissistic or self-absorbed, knowing that they are actually divisive. We can refuse to connect to anyone or any group that does not maintain a SOUL-full directive. Then we can connect to and support pages and news feeds from groups or individuals who have a United Life Generating Love Directed focus. This will be extraordinarily powerful. One by one, we will change the face of social media to evolve and grow all of us. And that would enable fantastic Constructive Collective Energy.

We can use what is to create what needs to be.

The real voyage of discovery consists not in seeking new landscapes, but in having new eyes.
Marcel Proust

It is also important that we don't become despondent when we see some remaining in Destructive patterns and 'buying' Destructive SOUL Food. When we are SOUL Directed, we are no longer affected by what others do. We are able to see those who connect to these Destructive Subliminal Connections compassionately, knowing they are lost in an Illusionary Self state. We are able to let them know the reasons for our choices, sharing the truth with them, without expectation.

Together we have examined only a few examples of ways in which we can become disconnected from our power and dis-abled by the Connections we make in 'norm-all' society. Many delusive Subliminal Connections keep us trapped in an Illusionary Self state. But when we choose our power, fulfillment, purpose, meaning and our future, and we know that it depends entirely on the connections we choose to make, or not make, we will create an underground movement that will eventually reshape reality. It's actually as simple as a focus: what you focus on grows, and what we, as a united group focus on grows exponentially.

This Condensed Version of the message is limited in how many examples it can provide. However, the underlying theme remains the same. And once we are Source Connected, we can see the patterns clearly, reappearing in many variations. We can see what matters and we can then do, say and be what matters.

Thank you for being the magnificent force you are!

The future enters into us, in order to transform itself in us, long before it happens.
Rainer Marie Rilke

3.2

Driving the Movement

To drive this movement all you need to do, and all you can do is know *who you really are*, hold on to your Core Self, retain a SOUL focus, and trust the magnificent unfolding that only a connection to the Source of All Life can enable. Simply do, say and be all you can to spread Love and a SOUL-full focus.

Be very careful about your connections and avoid Illusionary Self trappings. Remind your Self that now you see the world around you clearly, so you will clearly know what to do. Trust your Self.

Then understand your power. Don't forget that every little tiny thing you do, say, think and be matters. Remember Lorenz's "butterfly effect" which we discussed in Part One (1.2.6), and know that each action, thought and feeling has an enormous effect on the Energy of the world you live in. Feeling small, cynical or complacent is only going to disconnect you from all that matters and reduce your power to generate change.

A tiny change today brings a dramatically different tomorrow.
Richard Bach

Please also know that through you being part of this message, through you reading, speaking about and sharing The Truth, you are driving incredible change and creating a new reality. You are re-languaging the world as we know it, and you are manifesting and establishing a super freeway into *I'm-possibility* never seen before and never even imagined by mankind.

It's a very exciting time to be alive.

However, before we complete our conversation, taking our eternal union, our connection and the Ultimate Freedom Force we are generating into the world together, we need to take a quick look at where we are right now.

If what we focus on grows, let's look at the predominant focus in our world today. Then, we can adjust it to create a new world.

Never doubt that a small group of committed citizens can change the world.
Indeed, it is the only thing that ever has.
Margaret Mead

3.2.1   The Way the Current World Works

You may wonder why a small corporate, media, political minority are brainwashing and influencing us towards an empty, unfulfilled and often even sickening Illusionary Self state. Wouldn't they want us to be connected to that which empowers us and fulfills us? If not, then why not? Well, the truth is the world we live in today is ruled by a very effective system. And essentially that's an Economic System.

The Economic System is dominated by a select group of Corporations, owned by an exceptionally wealthy few. They have a vested economic interest in just about every major industry, political party and media group. The Economic System is based on an exchange of currency, called money. So the system's success depends on a Monetary System. And in simple terms, the more money that changes hands the 'healthier' the system is considered to be, and the wealthier those few who dictate the system become. Within this system, monetary wealth equals power.

There is a measure for the exchange of money that happens when we produce or purchase goods or services, which we then go on to 'sell' or 'buy'. This is called Gross Domestic Product (GDP) and today, in our current world, a country is only considered as important or 'successful' as it's GDP growth: the greater the GDP, the greater the country's power and influence.

At the moment, we have become part of this system, and like cogs in a wheel of a great machine, we keep the system running. Without you and I feeding and supporting the system, it would break down.

For the system to work efficiently, we need to spend money. We need to consume. So we become consumers. We need to keep buying as much as possible in order to generate GDP growth. In the West, we go to work. We work hard to get a pay rise, promotion, increase 'performance' or generate more 'profit'. We come home, usually exhausted. We buy food, clothes, cars, houses and a variety of things to go in them. We borrow money from banks, and that keeps us committed to working hard every day. We watch television, listen to the radio and read magazines in our 'leisure time', where we are consistently persuaded to believe in what depletes us, to spend more money and admire those who do. We are led to believe that extravagant spending on unnecessary things is a mark of success and prestige. And all of this keeps the Economic System thriving.

Normal is getting dressed in clothes that you buy for work
and driving through traffic in a car that you are still paying for
— in order to get to the job you need to pay for the clothes and the car,
and the house you leave vacant all day so you can afford to live there.
Ellen Goodman

The problem is this system – and the way of life that goes with it – connects us to our Illusionary Self. It completely disconnects us from *who we really are*, and from our joy and vitality.

We may survive, but we cannot possibly thrive while we are mechanized by an Economic System.

3.2.2 How Systems within the System Can Delude Us

Often what we are told we 'need', and what we are led to believe makes us well, is actually feeding the Economic System, and making us sick – very sick. We are affected not just at a SOUL level, but at a physical level as well.

Below are some challenging but vital facts, which provide only a few examples of how we can be misdirected by a SOUL-less Monetary System. This is not about singling out one or two systems within the larger system. It's about illustrating, through example, how Destructive an Economic System can be, even within the Health and Mental Health sector which we expect to support our wellbeing.

Before we begin this segment, and because we are about to discuss the Medical System, we need to first acknowledge the fact that doctors are some of the most genuine, caring people we could ever meet. They are usually deeply connected to a sense of great goodness. They are typically well-intended individuals, carrying a great desire to help others and to make a difference. And they do. They perform incredible, life-saving work daily. They give countless people life, and quality of life. They could, in many ways, be seen as the ultimate Life-Generators. Nurses, other medical professionals, and all those who care for us when we are sick or injured, enable and support life. For this reason, the genuinely 'good' people who work in the field of medicine and healthcare deserve the utmost respect and admiration.

This is an important point to make, and a vital point to remember as we travel ahead, because what is about to be discussed involves parts of the Medical System – and it is in no way intended to hurt, harm or misrepresent the wonderfully inspiring and impassioned people who work within this system. It simply provides a powerful illustration of how the systems-within-the-system control and dominate all of us, even those of us who are most well-intentioned.

Let us see this exploration for what it truly is – a reflection of where we are as people: a powerful Collective Reflection.

Let's start by looking at a couple of facts regarding Breast Cancer. Few of us realize that Breast Cancer Awareness Month (BCAM) is a billion dollar industry and bestselling brand that was created and is funded by a company who also manufactures the world's number one breast cancer treatment drug (Isaacs, T. 2009). And this drug has been proven to *cause* Breast Cancer (Natural News, 2009). Another interesting breast cancer fact is the *National Cancer Institute* itself declares that mammography could cause 75 cases of breast cancer for every 15 it identifies (Natural News, 2005).

It's worth noting that John D. Rockefeller is one of the elite super wealthy who control the Economic System, and he founded The American Cancer Society in 1913, the same year he established the Food and Drug Administration (FDA). The FDA will only approve patentable drugs – which means natural medicine that is available to all of us, and that is not a patentable chemical, cannot be approved by the FDA. John D. Rockefeller interestingly chose to take only natural and herbal remedies wherever possible, refusing pharmaceutical drugs himself.

Let food be thy medicine and medicine be thy food.
Hippocrates

Another disturbing fact is it is estimated that each chemotherapy patient is worth between US$250,000 - 500,000 to 'Big Pharma', a nickname for the large pharmaceutical companies (Bollinger, T. 2006, 2011). So perhaps it shouldn't surprise us that if GDP growth is the main focus in our Economic System, then the companies and organizations we are led to believe cure cancer and promote cancer awareness and fundraising, also cause it. In fact, with an Economic System focus, it may not even surprise us if Universities and Medical Schools are funded, and as a result doctors are trained, or indoctrinated, by these same organizations. And this is not the doctors' fault. They are simply part of the system.

One study published by the US National Library of Medicine National Institute of Health stated, "The overall contribution of curative and adjuvant cytotoxic chemotherapy to 5-year survival in adults was estimated to be 2.3% in Australia and 2.1% in the USA." Cytotoxic means 'cell killing'. The report went on to state, "To justify the continued funding and availability of drugs used in cytotoxic chemotherapy, a rigorous evaluation of the cost-effectiveness and impact on quality of life is urgently required" (Morgan, G., et al, 2004). No such publicized evaluation has occurred to date, yet we still continue to use these 'cell killing' treatments. Could it be because this is a very profitable industry that is very good for the health of our Economic System?

It can be very difficult and confronting to ask these questions and to Open our SOUL and eyes to what could really be happening, or to what we could be unintentionally growing and supporting. However, as challenging as it is, once we see the truth we will have pushed through that cocoon, and we will begin the route to our freedom. While we allow our Selves to be deluded, we will remain in the dark, paralyzed by our true potential.

Facts do not cease to exist because they are ignored.
Aldoux Huxley

It is imperative that we resist the temptation to blame or condemn individuals. We need to maintain a big picture focus. And as more and more individuals awaken to the truth, the wheel will begin to turn in a different direction.

Medical professionals, like other Western System educated people, trust what they 'know' – they believe what they've been taught. Their options, given various scenarios, have been laid out through their systemized learning or training. And they trust the Medical System, probably even more than you or I do. Most of the time what they have learned serves them, and us, very well. It really does work. It restores us. It saves lives. Advances in medicine have been mind boggling, especially over the last century. And this knowledge is powerful. But unfortunately, with this kind of power, the opportunity to generate Destruction is high.

Assuming most of what doctors are taught 'works', then how will they know if they're taught something that doesn't work? How would they know if within the working mix lies great deception? How would they know if they have become tools of the system?

The medical staff who promote and carry out the treatment, the ladies selling pink ribbons, the nurses injecting toxins into your veins, the journalist singing the praises of the charity – they're all doing what they're told is 'good' and 'right'. They are operating within a powerful, and complex system. They are not 'bad'. In fact they are good people doing what they believe is good and important work, unaware of the fact that they may have become cogs in a wheel.

The fact is cancer was virtually unknown a century ago and now it has reached epidemic proportions affecting one in three of us. Clearly something is happening, and it's not serving our health well.

If people let the government decide what foods they eat and what medicines they take,
their bodies will soon be in as a sorry state as the souls who live under tyranny.
Thomas Jefferson

Let's move on to our mental health. The occurrence of 'mental illness' is rising at increasingly rapid rates in today's world. Incredibly, it is much more prevalent in privileged society, or wealthy 'first world' countries than it is in underprivileged 'third world', or even war torn, countries. Common sense immediately brings into question an agenda based on this fact alone.

Perhaps it has something to do with the fact that the combined gross income from just the top five psychotropic drugs is higher than the total gross national product of over half the countries on earth. "Psychotropic drugs" are chemical drugs that affect or alter a person's mental state. In dollar terms this amounts to around a trillion dollars (that's $330 billion) each year (Citizens Commission on Human Rights, 2012). And just as a point of interest that's over ten times the amount of money required to eradicate global poverty completely, or to "completely solve global food insecurity" (Food and Agriculture Organization, United Nations' (FAO) 2008).

Maybe we are not as sick as we think we are. In fact, is it possible perhaps that these chemicals could be making us sick? Why are people in far worse circumstances not suffering from depression and mental illness like we are? Could it have anything to do with the profit involved when you or I use, and potentially become dependent upon, these mind altering chemicals – 'buying' them for the rest of our lives potentially? After all, if we are cogs in the wheel of an Economic System, which thrives when billions of dollars are sifted through it, then surely that makes sense.

Consider for a moment the fact that 10.6 million children die each year before they reach five years of age – that's the entire child population of France, Germany, Greece and Italy (Global Issues, 2010). And the money spent on alcohol consumption in Europe could provide basic education, clean water, reproductive health for women and basic health and nutrition for all people on our globe *2.6 times over* (Global Issues, 2010).

You see, the problem is every year 86% of the world's resources is consumed by 20% of the world's population (The Club of Budapest, Canada). What this means is the production and sale of weapons and war paraphernalia, or drugs sold to Westerners, for example, are profitable – these things grow GDP, they feed the Economic System.

So within this Economic System model it makes sense to keep us sick, or even make us sick, to encourage us to buy drugs just as it is beneficial to promote a war agenda. Within this system it makes no sense to invest money into those who are suffering and dying from poverty – this cannot grow GDP.

You may have heard of a reference source called the Diagnostic and Statistical Manual (DSM). Nicknamed the "Psychiatrists Bible", it is a manual published by the American Psychiatric Association used by psychiatrists and general practitioners to prescribe mental health drugs. The DSM lists symptoms and criteria, which are often very general and vague, in order to validate a mental illness diagnoses and treatment. Once a condition is 'diagnosed' through the DSM, the doctor can prescribe the appropriate psychotropic drug.

Amongst some of the disturbing facts regarding this DSM is it has no scientific or research criteria. It is simply a platform from which diseases and mental illnesses can be invented and determined, via the *votes* of a *selected board*. According to a Harvard University ethics center study, 69% of this board (currently called the DSM-5's taskforce) have personal financial ties to pharmaceutical companies (Cosgrove and Krimsky, 2012). In other words, those *creating* diagnosable mental 'illnesses' have a vested (personal financial) interest in the drug used to 'treat' the 'illness'. So, the easier they make it for doctors and psychiatrists to prescribe these 'medications' for *ordinary people* experiencing natural life conditions, the richer they get: *and* the more perks, special treatment – and most ironically, acclamation – they receive from those at the 'top' of their field.

Pharmaceutical companies pay psychiatrists to write articles promoting the use of their drugs. They also treat doctors and psychiatrists to flamboyant and extravagant "conferences", accommodating them in luxurious resorts in exotic locations in order to drive business.

So hardly surprisingly the current DSM lists almost 400 'mental illnesses', which is more than three times what was listed only forty years ago. The revised DSM-5 has controversially contrived some ridiculous 'disorders' such as "Prolonged Grief Disorder" which explains itself as such: "grief reactions of more than *two weeks* may be diagnosed as depression" (The Guardian, 2012). This would validate the use of psychotropic drugs whenever we experience loss, which is a natural part of the process of life. Whatever happened to feeling our feelings in this scenario? Not only would we be unable to heal through the process of sadness and sense of loss that comes with grief, but we would be prescribed drugs that permanently alter our brain chemistry, sabotaging our healing process as well as our overall health – perhaps for a lifetime.

Even the natural process of memory loss in the elderly, or the tantrum phase in our vulnerable children are being considered as forms of 'mental illnesses' requiring dangerous mind-altering chemicals which commonly develop a lifetime dependence in their users.

The majority suffer, usually ignorantly, so a minority can benefit. This is how the Economic System works, regardless of the 'Industry'.

The truth is the Cancer and the Mental Health 'Industries' are amongst the most profitable in the world today, so why would finding a cure for cancer, or promoting a fulfilling lifestyle and focus, be desirable if economic growth is the real focus over saving lives?

These examples have been used because they apply to the aspects of our life we value most – our mental and physical health. They are designed to wake us up out of our complacency. But they do not stand alone. They represent a pattern or structure within society that is evident everywhere. While an Economic System drives us and our focus, we will become slaves to it. We will lose our Selves. The human race and entire planet will disintegrate. And even those who become materially wealthy through this system will be empty and lost. No one wins.

We must change our focus.

We need to remember that before our awareness, we are all trapped in an Illusionary Self state. Regardless of our career, profession, training or qualifications, we have all been exposed to Subliminal Connections that keep us tapped into the system. So, in an autopilot state, and without awareness, we can be dominated and driven by that which destroys us.

It is in the system's interest to keep us all zombie-fied, and mechanized.

All of us, including teachers, policemen, solicitors, psychologists, pharmacists, bankers, economists, accountants, journalists and any other profession you care to name – are taught what we know through the system.

We are taught 'what' to think. In this system, 'how' to think exists only within the parameters of what is already known – what has been, is being, or is about to be, taught. This applies to every single one of us who are 'educated' in the current conventional Education System. We learn 'what' to think, without learning 'how' to think. And often we are called to action without being conscious to *who we really are*, and therefore without conscience. And that is how the Economic System drives good people to do unconscionable things.

We must ask questions. And we must see the truth, even though some truth can be very difficult to digest.

THE TRUTH AD INFINITUM

The truth does not change according to our ability to stomach it.
Flannery O'Connor

Often that which feeds and fuels GDP starves and destroys us.

Using the phenomenal Collective Energy we are now forming, we can unite in great numbers. Medical professionals who know the truth can band together using years of research and independent studies to truly prevent cancer, and educate people about the current treatments. Doctors, Psychologists and Psychiatrists who are awakened to the truth will be genuinely saving lives and creating a better world by unifying in a quest to no longer be dominated, manipulated and dictated to by the Pharmaceutical Industry. These people will be amongst our greatest heroes.

We simply need to band together, and to forge a new direction.

We can start independent Medical Schools that are not funded by the Pharmaceutical Industry. We can expose corruption and hidden agendas. We can apply the simple new language we have discovered together and do only that which is Life-Generating regardless of what the system dictates. We cannot be held hostage to a system unless we allow our Selves to be. And as more of us stand up to be counted, we will use the great advances we have made over the last century to benefit all of us.

We all need to be brave enough to see the truth. And when we see that what we're doing is Destructive and change what we're doing, we are in doing so changing the world.

I would unite with anybody to do right and with nobody to do wrong.
Frederick Douglass

3.2.3   We Hold the Power

In summary, within the Economic System there are many other systems which all support the same aim, agenda or focus, including a Political, Educational, Legal, Defense and Banking System. The media as well as the entertainment industry is used as a propaganda tool, to promote the system's aims or agenda. And the majority of us play into its hands, obliviously.

The result is a tiny minority of the world become increasingly rich and powerful. They dominate and control the rest of the world's population in whatever way works best for the Economic System. Corporations therefore rule the world. And we allow them to – simply by buying what they sell us.

Unfortunately though, by ignorantly buying into the system we are selling our Selves very short.

The truth is we hold the power, despite what we are led to believe. We are the mechanism of every single system within the greater system. Every system depends entirely on you and I for its survival. And when we change our focus and sentiment, we will also change what we do, buy, and believe. Then the system will have to adjust, to us. Therefore we control the system. It does not control us.

When we change what we connect to we will change the world.

The point is you have now uncovered *who you really are*. You know you are unlimited, infinite Life-Generating Energy at your Elemental Core. And you know that to be Love Directed and Life Generating will be your ultimate feeder. This is your life purpose. You also know that to be this powerful Essence enables you to live and experience unimaginable magnificence.

Even though you are currently living in a system that is designed, in many ways, to diminish you and keep you in an Illusionary Self state of servitude, your newfound vision will allow you to take the reins back.

A small body of determined spirits fired by an unquenchable faith in their mission can alter the course of history.
Mahatma Gandhi

The truth is war, weapons, drugs, prisons, disease and even poverty campaigns are incredibly profitable. Corporations, politicians and the media work together to generate income. Often they promote what makes us sick under the guise of what makes us well.

We simply need to remain aware, connected to our Source Self, and we need to refuse to believe everything we are told.

Then, we need to trust our inner knowing, our instinct and the greater power within us, treading deliberately and determinedly in the direction of our dreams.

See if you can do all you can to carefully select and engage in only that which is Life-Generating. If you are confused, ask questions. Allow your Self to be supported and encouraged by those who have joined the truth revolution. As we unite and grow in a committed Life Generating focus, we will notice new paths unfolding, like magic. As we refuse to consume what consumes us, we will evolve individually and as One, transforming our Selves, one another and the world around us.

Start doing the things you think should be done,
and start being what you think society should become.
Do you believe in free speech? Then speak freely.
Do you love the truth? Then tell it.
Do you believe in an open society? Then act in the open.
Do you believe in a decent and humane society?
Then behave decently and humanely.
Adam Michnik

3.3

Together Forever

The incredible reality is that once you are connected to the ultimate Source of All Life, of everything that is and of all that can be, you realize you are not driving this movement. It is driving itself, just as all life is created, one connection at a time, in the most baffling and inconceivable ways.

We simply need to remain connected to only that which generates all life. Then we will be carried with, through and by the ultimate series of splendid and awe-inspiring connections. And we will land in a realm of reality that is currently beyond the bounds of possibility.

The secret is to hold on to who you really are, and then just trust.

Allow your Self to be moved and motivated by the most spectacular Life Force. Allow your Individual Energy to be part of the greatest Collective Energy in the universe.

You have already begun the ultimate personal and universal evolution. Together, you and I have already stepped firmly into a new future, one that is already permanently changed. We have begun the transformation of the human race. We have started a new growth pattern, expanded our Selves, and altered the course of history. It has already happened. The arrival of this message has already changed the world.

And incredible change will continue to happen. It will happen at an increasing rate, as more people discover the only way forward. We, you and I, and all those who join us in this – our ultimate freedom plight – will adapt together, forming a new type of humankind. We will change the very cells in our body, and in our collective body of existence. We have already metamorphosed. And we will continue to develop the most incredible revelation, evolution and revolution ever.

We have united through the greatest Life Force that resides within us all. WE are One. And that is an eternal connection. You are part of my Energy, and I am part of yours. We are evermore connected for the good of one another and for the good of all.

Thank you for joining the discussion on the website that goes with this message. Thank you for spreading the word in whatever way feels right to you. As you do all you can, all you can be will be. Feel free to expand your journey through the Original Version of this message, which provides a more detailed step-by-step process of discovery with stories and examples of applied knowledge. But most of all, please honor the incredible, perpetual, glorious ever-evolving, miraculous Force you are. Never forget what a divinely spectacular phenomenon of Life you are.

Thank you for changing the world.

The day the power of love overrules the love of power,
the world will know peace.
Gandhi

Every nation must now develop an overriding loyalty to mankind as a whole
in order to preserve the best in their individual societies.
This call for a worldwide fellowship
that lifts neighborly concern beyond one's tribe, race, class, and nation
is in reality a call for an all-embracing and
unconditional love for all mankind...
...When I speak of love
I am not speaking of some sentimental and weak response.
I am not speaking of that force which is just emotional bosh.
I am speaking of that force which all of the great religions have seen
as the supreme unifying principle of life
Love is somehow the key that unlocks the door
which leads to the ultimate reality.

Martin Luther King Jr.

Author's Note

Connected ad infinitum…

So here we are
at the end of our journey together
through the Condensed Version
of this vital message.
But like all 'ends' this is actually a new beginning.
And this is the greatest beginning of all time.

You, me, and all who join us,
will be part of the greatest revolution on earth.
We have already begun the revelation.
We will be responsible for generating
the most incredible and unimaginable reality.
We will change the course of history.
There is nothing more splendid than that.

This is not a utopian dream.
We have joined forces now
and we are forevermore linked,
both consciously and subconsciously.
We have formed a new focus,
and in doing so, we have already begun a new reality.

Feel within you
the wonderful inner strength
that comes with understanding who you really are,
what really matters and
knowing we have one another as Energetic partners
in creating the reality we so deeply crave.

Feel within you
the fantastic inner peace
that comes with knowing how deeply you are loved and appreciated
by me, and by all those who value the future of our world.

THE TRUTH AD INFINITUM

Feel within you
the astounding power
that comes with knowing and feeling the great connection
to your Inner Soul,
to the Inner Soul of all,
and to the Greatest Life Force in the Universe.

You are forever changed.
WE are forever connected.
Together Forever
we are set to make history!
Yours with abundant and eternal Gratitude and Love,

AD Infinitum

Imagine

Imagine there's no heaven
It's easy if you try
No hell below us
Above us only sky
Imagine all the people
Living for today…

Imagine there're no countries
It isn't hard to do
Nothing to kill or die for
And no religion too
Imagine all the people
Living life in peace…

You may say I'm a dreamer
But I'm not the only one
I hope some day you'll join us
And the world will be as one

Imagine no possessions
I wonder if you can
No need for greed or hunger
A brotherhood of man
Imagine all the people
Sharing all the world…

You may say I'm a dreamer
But I'm not the only one
I hope some day you'll join us
And the world will live as one

John Lennon

Quote References

PART ONE

Aristotle (384 –322 BC) was an Ancient Greek philosopher, physicist and poet. His views are believed to have shaped Western philosophy.
Bible, Holy (NIV) The New International Version (NIV) of the Holy Bible is an original translation of the Bible, based on the work of over one hundred scholars. The Bible is a collection of sacred Judaism and Christian texts.
Blake, William (1757-1827) was a (sometimes prophetic) English poet and human rights campaigner. Although unrecognised while he was alive, he is now considered a seminal figure in the Romantic Age. This is the first verse of the poem "Auguries of Innocence" in which Blake portrays the world as entirely interconnected.
Buddha (c.563 BCE or c.480 BCE-c.483 BCE or c. 400 BCE) is the Founder of Buddhism.
Democritus (460 BC-370 BC) was an influential Ancient Greek philosopher and atomic theorist.
Dimitrov (1999-2003) was a highly regarded Chaos and Complexity Theorist.
Einstein, Albert (1879-1955) is regarded the most influential physicist of the 20th century.
Frankl, Victor (1905-1997) was a famous Austrian Professor of Neurology and Psychiatry, Neurologist and Holocaust survivor. An internationally speaker, honorary lecturer and best-selling author, with over 32 books, his most famous publication was *Man's Search for Meaning*.
Gandhi, Mohandas Karamchand, known as Mahatma Gandhi, (1869-1948) inspired freedom through peace as he led India to independence through non-violent civil disobedience.
The Guru Granth Sahib, also known as the Adi Granth, is the Sikhism religious scripture. It combined the writings of Gurus and saints from a variety of religions.
McTaggart, Lynne (born 1951) is an American author, journalist and lecturer.
Pierre Teilhard de Chardin (1881-1955) was a French Jesuit priest and philosopher.
Ramakrishna (1863-1886) was a famous Indian mystic, who believed all religions lead to the same God.
Ramana Maharshi (1879-1950) was a Hindu spiritual master.

Rilke, Rainer Maria (1875-1926) was a famous best-selling Austrian poet, novelist and philosopher.
Swami Paramananda (1884-1940) was an Indian mystic and spiritual leader.
Rumi (1207-1273) was an evolutionary and revolutionary Persian Muslim poet and Sufi mystic.

PART TWO

Aristotle (384 –322 BC) was an Ancient Greek philosopher, physicist and poet. His views are believed to have shaped a profound understanding of philosophy.
Bell, Alexander Graham (1847-1922) was an eminent Scottish scientist who is credited with the invention of the telephone.
Buddha (563-483 BC) Hindu Prince Gautama Siddharta, the founder of Buddhism.
Carver, George Washington (1864-1943) was an inspiring American scientist, botanist, educator, inventor and writer who was originally born into slavery.
Cayce, Edgar (1877-1945) was an eminent American prophet who is believed to have given answers to life's big questions while in a hypnotic trance. His messages focused prominently on healing and the sick.
Chinmoy, Sri (1931-2007), born Chinmoy Kumar Chose, was an Indian spiritual Master, author, poet, meditation teacher and interfaith leader.
Gandhi, Mahatma - born Mohandas Karamchand Gandhi (1869-1948) inspired freedom through peace as he led India to independence through non-violent civil disobedience.
Einstein, Albert (1879-1955) is regarded the most influential physicist of the 20th century.
Ehrmann, Max (1872-1945) was a famous American attorney, writer and poet.
Epicetus (AD 55-AD 135) was a Greek philosopher.
Hiley, Basil (born 1953) is a University of London professor emeritus quantum physicist. He was awarded the "Best Person in Physics" Majorana Prize in 2012.
King, Martin Luther, Jr. (1929-1968) was a prominent African-American Civil Rights activist, clergyman and leader.
Lewis, Clive Staples (1898-1963) was a great internationally acclaimed Irish Christian novelist and academic, most famous for *The Chronicles of Narnia.*
Maharshi, Ramana (1879-1950) was a Hindu spiritual master.

Mother Teresa (1910-1997) was a Roman Catholic sister and Nobel Peace Prize recipient who provided and ran hospices, homes, orphanages, schools and soup kitchens for the most vulnerable.

Rilke, Rainer Maria (1875-1926) was a famous best-selling Austrian poet, novelist and philosopher.

Rumi (1207-1273) was an evolutionary and revolutionary Persian Muslim poet and Sufi mystic.

Searls, David (born 1947) is an American journalist, technology writer and author.

Sophocles (496-406BC) was an ancient Greek playwriter.

Stafford, William (1914-1993) was a American poet and pacifist.

Tzu, Lao (600BC-531BC) was a famous Chinese philosopher, and founder of Taoism. He wrote *Tao Te Ching.*

PART THREE

Bach, Richard (born 1937) is an American author best known for best selling timeless classic "Jonathon Livingston Seagull", which provides a thoughtful metaphor for society.

Bible, Holy (NIV) The New International Version (NIV) of the Holy Bible is an original translation of the Bible, based on the work of over one hundred scholars. The Bible is a collection of sacred Judaism and Christian texts.

Buddha (563-483 BC) Hindu Prince Gautama Siddharta was the founder of Buddhism.

Douglass, Frederick (1818-1895) was an African-American writer, antislavery campaigner and social rights reformer who promoted equality for all people.

Edison, Thomas (1847-1931) was a brilliant scientist, most famous for inventing the electric light bulb.

Einstein, Albert (1879-1955) is regarded the most influential physicist of the 20th century.

Gandhi, Mahatma (1869-1948) Mohandas Karamchand Gandhi was an inspirational leader and social change activist who led India to independence through non-violent civil disobedience, peace and truth.

Goodman, Ellen (born 1941) is a Pulitzer Prize-winning author and social commentator.

Hippocrates (c. 460-c.370 BC) was a revolutionary Greek physician, founder of the Hippocratic School of Medicine, nicknamed the "Father of Medicine".

Hopper, Grace Murray (1906-1992) was a pioneering American computer scientist.

Huxley, Aldoux (1894-1963) was an English philosopher, humanist, pacifist, Universalist and writer, most famous for his classic novel "Brave New World".

Jefferson, Thomas (1743-1826) was the third President of the United States.

King, Martin Luther, Jr. (1929-1968) was a Nobel Peace Prize recipient and prominent leader in the African-American Civil Rights Movement. He achieved freedoms and rights for a poor and oppressed majority through non-violent civil disobedience.

Lennon, John (1940-1980) was a British musician, singer, songwriter and member of "The Beatles" who was also an avid peace activist.

Mead, Margaret (1901-1978) was an American author, anthropologist and speaker awarded the Presidential Medal of Freedom in honor of her life.

Michnik, Adam (born 1946) is a Polish Jewish author and historian, who was imprisoned for his courage to stand up for freedoms and against communism. He was awarded a Knight of Legion of Honor and European of the Year award.

O'Connor, Flannery (1925-1964) was an American writer and novelist.

Paramananda, Swami (1884-1940) was a renowned Indian mystic and spiritual leader.

Proust, Marcel (1871-1922) was a famous French novelist and writer.

Rilke, Rainer Maria (1875-1926) was an internationally acclaimed best-selling Austrian poet, novelist and philosopher.

Shaw, George Bernard (1856-1950) was a Nobel Prize winning Irish writer, playwright, journalist and social rights activist who campaigned for equality and against exploitation.

Twain, Mark (1835-1910) Samuel Langhorne Clemens - pen name Mark Twain - was an American author and social activist against slavery, best known for "The Adventures of Tom Sawyer".

Zinn, Howard (1922-2010) was an award-winning professor, social rights and peace campaigner, best-selling author, playwright and social activist whose aim was to give people power and hope.

References and Further Reading

PART ONE

Bible, Holy (NIV) The New International Version (NIV) of the Holy Bible is an original translation of the Bible, based on the work of over one hundred scholars. The Bible is a collection of sacred Judaism and Christian texts.

Bohm, D., Hiley, B.J. (1993) *The Undivided Universe: An ontological interpretation of quantum theory.* London: Routledge

Bress, E. & Mackye Gruber, J. (2004) *The Butterfly Effect.* New Line Cinema: USA, Canada.

Dimitrov, V. (2003) *Autopoiesis in Organisations.* University of Western Sydney, Hawkesbury Campus, Australia. Retrieved September 10, 2009, from

http://www.zulenet.com/VladimirDimitrov/default.html

Frankl, V. (2006) *Man's Search for Meaning.* Beacon Press.

Gerhardt, S. (2004) *Why Love Matters.* Brunner-Routledge: New York, London

Gilligan, J. (1997) *Violence: Reflections on a National Epidemic.* Vinatage.

Grille, R. (2005) *Parenting for a Peaceful World.* Longueville Media: Sydney

Kuhn, L. (2009) *Adventures in Complexity: For Organisations Near the Edge of Chaos.* Station Offices. Aximinster. Devon, UK: Triarchy Press

Lorenz, E. (1995) The Essence of Chaos. CRC Press.

Maslow, A.H. (1943) *A Theory of Human Motivation*: Hierarchy of Needs. Psychological Review: 50 (4), 370-96.

Maslow, A.H. (1970) *Motivation and Personality.* Harper and Row: New York.

Mate, G. (2010) *In the Realm of Hungry Ghosts.* Random House Knopf: Canada.

Pribram, Karl (1991) *Brain and Perception: Holonomy and Structure in Figural Processing.* Lawrence Erlbaum Associates.

Talbot, M. (1991) *The Holographic Universe.* Harper Perennial. New York.

Wilkinson, R. G. (2011) *The Spirit Level: Why Greater Equality Makes Societies Stronger.* Bloomsbury Press.

PART TWO

Bohm, D., Hiley, B.J. (1993) *The Undivided Universe: An ontological interpretation of quantum theory*. London: Routledge
Sri Dhammananda, K. (1989) *How to Live Without Fear and Worry*. Kuala Lumpur, Malaysia. Buddhist Missionary Society.
Moorjani, A. (2012) *Dying to be Me*. Hay House.
Rilke, R.M. (2008) *Letters to a Young Poet*. BN Publishing.

PART THREE

Bach, R. (2014) Jonathan Livingston Seagull. (first published in 1970 by Macmillan) Scribner; Reissue edition.
Bible, Holy (NIV) The New International Version (NIV) of the Holy Bible is an original translation of the Bible, based on the work of over one hundred scholars. The Bible is a collection of sacred Judaism and Christian texts.
Bollinger, T. M. (2006) *Cancer: Step Outside the Box*. (Updated 2011) Infinity 510 Squared Partners.
Citizens Commission on Human Rights: Watchdog Investigating and Exposing Psychiatric Human Rights Violations. *Making a Killing: The Untold Story of Psychotropic Drugs*. Retrieved 5 April, 2012 from http://www.cchr.org/videos/making-a-killing.html
The Club of Budapest, Canada. *World Facts and Trends*. Retrieved 20th November, 2012, from http://www.clubofbudapest.ca/World_Facts_-101226.html
Cosgrove, L., Krimsky, S. (2012) Open Access. *Comparison of DSM-IV and DSM-5 Panel Members' Financial Associations with Industry: A Pernicious Problem Exists*. Retrieved 28th August, 2012, from http://www.ncbi.nlm.nih.gov/pmc/articles/PMC3302834/pdf/pmed.1001190.pdf
Food and Agriculture Organization (2008) *The World Only Needs 30 Billion Dollars a Year to Eradicate the Scourge of Hunger*. Retrieved 28th May, 2012, from http://www.fao.org/Newsroom/en/news/2008/1000853/index.html
Gladwell, M. (2002) *The Tipping Point*. Back Bay Books.
Global Issues (2010) *Poverty Facts and Stats*. Retrieved 20th November, 2012 from http://www.globalissues.org/article/26/poverty-facts-and-stats#src1
Guardian, The (2012) *Grief is Good News for Pharmaceutical Companies*. Retrieved 28th August, 2012 from

http://www.guardian.co.uk/society/2012/aug/14/grief-good-news-big-pharma

Isaacs, T. (2009) *Breast Cancer Deception – Hiding the Truth Beneath a Sea of Pink*. Retrieved 28th August, 2012 from http://www.naturalnews.com/027300_cancer_breast_health.html

Korten, D.C (2001) *When Corporations Rule the World*. Berrett-Koehler Publishers.

Morgan, G., Ward, R., Barton, M. (2004) PubMed.gov. *US National Library of Medicine National Institute of Health: The Contribution of Cytotoxic Chemotherapy to 5-year Survival in Adult Malignancies*. Department of Radiation Oncology, Northern Sydney Cancer Centre, Royal North Shore Hospital, Sydney, NSW, Australia. gmorgan@bigpond.net.au. Retrieved 27th August, from http://www.ncbi.nlm.nih.gov/pubmed/15630849?ordinalpos=1&itool=EntrezSystem2.PEntrez.Pubmed.Pubmed_ResultsPanel.Pubmed_RVDocSum

NaturalNews.com (2005) *Mammograms Cause Breast Cancer (and other cancer facts you probably never knew)*. Retrieved 27th August, 2012 from http://www.naturalnews.com/010886_breast_cancer_mammograms.html

NaturalNews.com (2009) *Long-term Tamoxifen Use Increases Risk of Aggressive Breast Cancer*. September 28, 2009. Retrieved 11th May, 2015 from http://www.naturalnews.com/027123_cancer_Tamoxifen_risk.html

NaturalNews.com (2009) *Mammograms Cause Breast Cancer, Groundbreaking New Research Declares*. Retrieved 27th August, 2012 from http://www.naturalnews.com/027641_mammograms_breast_cancer.html

World Hunger Education Service (2015) *2015 World Hunger and Poverty Facts and Statistics*. Retrieved March 30, 2015, from www.worldhunger.org

YouTube (2010) Uploaded by Derek Sivers. *First Follower: Leadership Lessons from Dancing Guy*. Downloaded 2 April, 2015 from www.youtube.com.

Zinn, H. (2004) *Howard Zinn: You Can't Be Neutral on a Moving Train*. Documentary. Directed by Deb Ellis and Denis Mueller.

www.ingramcontent.com/pod-product-compliance
Lightning Source LLC
Chambersburg PA
CBHW071529040426
42452CB00008B/937